Autoimmunities

Autoimmunity refers to the phenomenon whereby an organism or body mounts an immune response against its own tissues. As a medical term, autoimmunity is today used to account for any instance in which the body fails to recognise its own constituents as 'self', an error that results in the paradoxical situation in which self-defense (immunity, protection) manifests as self-harm (pathology). As a result, the very possibility of autoimmunity poses a problem for the notion of immunity and the concept of identity that underpins it: if self-protection can just as readily take the form of self-destruction, then it seems that the very identity of the self, and thus the boundary between self and other, is in question. Conceptually, autoimmunity thus challenges us to think critically about the nature of any sovereign entity or identity, be they human or nonhuman, cells, nations, or other forms of community.

This volume reflects and engages with different disciplinary approaches to autoimmunity in the theoretical, medical or posthumanities, social and political theory, and critical science studies. It aims to provide a topical intervention within the current discussion on biopolitical thought and critical posthumanist futures.

This book was originally published as a special issue of *Parallax.*

Stefan Herbrechter is a research fellow at Coventry University, UK; a Privatdozent at Heidelberg University, Germany; and general editor of criticalposthumanism.net.

Michelle Jamieson is a sociologist and lecturer in the Faculty of Arts at Macquarie University, Australia.

Autoimmunities

Edited by
Stefan Herbrechter and Michelle Jamieson

Routledge
Taylor & Francis Group
LONDON AND NEW YORK

First published 2018
by Routledge
2 Park Square, Milton Park, Abingdon, Oxon, OX14 4RN, UK

and by Routledge
711 Third Avenue, New York, NY 10017, USA

Routledge is an imprint of the Taylor & Francis Group, an informa business

British Library Cataloguing in Publication Data
A catalogue record for this book is available from the British Library

ISBN 13: 978-1-138-54230-3

Typeset in New Baskerville
by RefineCatch Limited, Bungay, Suffolk

Publisher's Note
The publisher accepts responsibility for any inconsistencies that may have arisen during the conversion of this book from journal articles to book chapters, namely the possible inclusion of journal terminology.

Disclaimer
Every effort has been made to contact copyright holders for their permission to reprint material in this book. The publishers would be grateful to hear from any copyright holder who is not here acknowledged and will undertake to rectify any errors or omissions in future editions of this book.

Contents

Citation Information

The chapters in this book were originally published in *Parallax*, volume 23, issue 1 (January–March 2017). When citing this material, please use the original page numbering for each article, as follows:

Chapter 1
Fortress
Stefan Herbrechter
Parallax, volume 23, issue 1 (January–March 2017), pp. 1–10

Chapter 2
Allergy and Autoimmunity: Rethinking the Normal and the Pathological
Michelle Jamieson
Parallax, volume 23, issue 1 (January–March 2017), pp. 11–27

Chapter 3
Self, Not-Self, Not Not-Self But Not Self, or The Knotty Paradoxes of 'Autoimmunity': A Genealogical Rumination
Ed Cohen
Parallax, volume 23, issue 1 (January–March 2017), pp. 28–45

Chapter 4
Autoimmunity: the political state of nature
Vicki Kirby
Parallax, volume 23, issue 1 (January–March 2017), pp. 46–60

Chapter 5
Cosmic Topologies of Imitation: From the Horror of Digital Autotoxicus to the Auto-Toxicity of the Social
Tony D. Sampson
Parallax, volume 23, issue 1 (January–March 2017), pp. 61–76

Chapter 6
Contagion, Virology, Autoimmunity: Derrida's Rhetoric of Contamination
Peta Mitchell
Parallax, volume 23, issue 1 (January–March 2017), pp. 77–93

Chapter 7

Auto (Immunity): Evolutions of Otherness
Nicole Anderson
Parallax, volume 23, issue 1 (January–March 2017), pp. 94–107

Chapter 8

(Auto)immunity, Social Theory, and the 'Political'
Cary Wolfe
Parallax, volume 23, issue 1 (January–March 2017), pp. 108–122

Notes on Contributors

Nicole Anderson is Head of the Media, Music, Communication and Cultural Studies Department at Macquarie University, Australia. Her most recent book is *Derrida: Ethics Under Erasure* (2012). She is the co-founder and co-editor of the journal *Derrida Today* and sole director of the Derrida Today Conferences.

Ed Cohen is professor of Women's and Gender Studies at Rutgers University, USA. He is the author of *A Body Worth Defending: Immunity, Biopolitics and the Apotheosis of the Modern Body* (2009).

Stefan Herbrechter is a research fellow at Coventry University, UK; a Privatdozent at Heidelberg University, Germany; and general editor of criticalposthumanism.net.

Michelle Jamieson is a sociologist and lecturer in the Faculty of Arts at Macquarie University, Australia.

Vicki Kirby is professor of Sociology and Anthropology at the University of New South Wales, Australia. She is the editor of *What If Culture Was Nature All Along?* (2017) and author of *Quantum Anthropologies: Life at Large* (2011), and *Judith Butler: Live Theory* (2006).

Peta Mitchell is a research fellow at the Queensland University of Technology, Australia. She is the author of *Cartographic Strategies of Postmodernity* (2008) and *Contagious Metaphor* (2012).

Tony D. Sampson is reader in Digital Cultures and Communication at the University of East London, UK. He is the author of *Virality: Contagion Theory in the Age of Networks* (Press, 2012) and *The Assemblage Brain: Sense Making in Neuroculture* (2017), and the editor of *Affect and Social Media* (with Ellis and Maddison, 2018).

Cary Wolfe is the Dunlevie Chair in English at Rice University, USA, and the director of The Center for Critical and Cultural Theory. His books include *Animal Rites: American Culture, The Discourse of Species, and Posthumanist Theory* (2003), the edited collection *Zoontologies: The Question of the Animal* (2003), and *Before the Law: Humans and Other Animals in a Biopolitical Frame* (2013).

Fortress

Stefan Herbrechter

Today immunity informs us deeply:
as organisms, as individuals, as citizens, and as a species.[2]

The price of an 'auto-' is an 'alter-' – there is no need for a notion of 'self' without a notion of 'other'. Thus far, things seem pretty 'safe': consciousness, knowledge, agency, in short: metaphysics, arises from this systemic (re)distribution. It was Emmanuel Levinas who saw the need for a 'desensitization' therapy for (Western) metaphysics through a revaluation of alterity and its 'precedence' over any self and identity:

> Western philosophy coincides with the disclosure of the other where the other, in manifesting itself as being, loses its alterity. From its infancy philosophy has been struck with a horror of the other that remains other – with an insurmountable allergy.[3]

In his epitaph on Levinas, Jacques Derrida turns the question of allergy into one of the guiding threads for reading Levinas' and his own work. For example, with regard to the hospitality of the other:

> The closing of the door, inhospitality, war, and allergy already imply, as their possibility, a hospitality offered or received: an

> original or, more precisely, pre-originary declaration of peace [...] For Levinas, on the contrary, allergy, the refusal or forgetting of the face, comes to inscribe its secondary negativity against a backdrop of peace, against the backdrop of a hospitality that does not belong to the order of the political, or at least not simply to a political space [...] the phenomena of allergy, rejection, xenophobia, even war itself would still exhibit everything that Levinas explicitly attributes to or allies with hospitality.[4]

Both Levinas and Derrida are aware that there is nothing reassuring in this insight of a necessary 'pre-originary hospitality'. This knowledge cannot prevent allergy, war or rejection of the other, but at least it forces one to open up or to disentangle and show possible ethical and political alternatives:

> War or allergy, the inhospitable rejection, is still derived from hospitality [...] In any event [...] allergy, the inhospitable forgetting of the transcendence of the Other [...] is still a testimony, an unconscious testimony ... to the very thing it forgets [...][5]

Allergies are thus something that 'we' have to learn to live with.

In his medical history of humanity, Roy Porter writes of a great surge in the interest in immunology in the late 1980s due to the discovery of AIDS.[6] David Napier presents the long term view of modernity as an 'age of immunology' and 'self-awareness', culminating in what he calls 'identity stasis'. He aims to provide 'an analysis of the ways in which "self" and an *internalized* "nonself" function: culturally, medically, scientifically'.[7] He sees immunology as a 'cultural paradigm' in which 'immunological ideas now provide the primary conceptual framework in which human relations take place in the contemporary world', which leads to an 'increasing *internalization of difference* within a presumably autonomous self', so that 'immunology – the attempted elimination of the internalized "other" – is projected everywhere'.[8] How does allergy and autoimmunity as the 'modern malady' *par excellence*[9] fit into this? Michelle Jamieson's contribution to this special issue provides some very helpful clarification in this respect and also offers a brief medical history of the concept of allergy.

By way of further explanation, in an introduction to a special issue of *Cultural Anthropology* on this issue, Napier explains:

> The origins of immunology as a medical discipline can easily be traced to the 19th century. But in the late 1960s the notion of an "immune system" first appeared, marking a conceptual shift in which immunity involved not only sensitive reactions to allergies and pathogens, but an orchestrated cellular defense in which complex responses protected an autonomous self. Since then, immunity has in broad terms come to be understood primarily as a dynamic process of recognizing and eliminating

> so-called "nonself." However, over the same period, immunologists have gradually grown dissatisfied with the general self-nonself construct as they grapple with the disjunction between what they evidence experimentally, and received ideas about organic preservation and the effects of "foreign" bodies on a self that is otherwise sovereign.[10]

This dissatisfaction resulting from a too simplistic view of the self-nonself binary opposition clinically but also culturally, politically, ethically and philosophically is prompted and exacerbated by the 'problem', question and phenomenon of autoimmunity. It is also the conundrum or aporia that, due to the ubiquity and power that the 'immunological' model of the 'sovereign self' has achieved, preoccupies, according to Napier, 'social constructions of personhood [...] and prevailing neoliberal ideas about individual autonomy'.[11] The counterintuitive notion of (self-)intolerant bodies, as Warwick Anderson and Ian Mackay explain, is 'still emerging, still to gain broad cultural acceptance'.[12]

> That the immune system, so much part of us, so necessary to survival, can go amiss and cause disease is counterintuitive. The body's failure to recognize itself, its capacity to treat itself as foreign, seems both sinister and bizarre.[13]

The associated 'immunological turn' that Anderson and Mackay identify is produced by the fact that 'autoimmunity has growing appeal to philosophers and social theorists as a guiding metaphor in understanding the perils of life and identity in the twenty-first century'.[14] A long list of influential contemporary thinkers (Sloterdijk, Derrida, Agamben, Esposito to name only the most prominent) have been extending the currency of notions of (auto)immunity and have been building bridges between medical science and cultural and political theory. According to Andrey Goffey, 'it is the aggressively imagistic *language* of security and warfare, which runs throughout the historical development of immunology, that has proved of most interest to critical researchers'.[15] He further relates this to the rise of the life sciences during the time of the Cold War and the contemporary return to questions of biopolitics.

Roberto Esposito, for example, claims that the 'demand for exemption or protection' the autoimmunity paradigm stands for has been 'extended to all those other sectors and languages of our life, until it becomes the coagulating point, both real and symbolic, of the entire contemporary experience'.[16] Likewise, Peter Sloterdijk understands modernity, globalization and the age of terror as 'the struggle to create [...] metaphorical space suits, immunitary regimes [...] that will protect Europeans from dangerous and life-threatening contact with the outside'.[17] Sloterdijk sees the process of 'hominization' precisely in this development of immunizing 'anthropotechnics', which, today, has reached the demand for 'global co-immunity' in the face of climate change and the advent of the 'posthuman'.

What remains unclear is the constant slippage from immunity to autoimmunity and back again in these contexts. An awareness of the inevitability of this slippage is probably Jacques Derrida's most important contribution within the emergence of the autoimmunitarian 'paradigm' in contemporary thought. Nicole Anderson, in her contribution to this issue, provides a recapitulation and a critique of the role of autoimmunity in Derrida's late work (from *Specters of Marx* and the *Politics of Friendship*, via *Faith and Knowledge* to *Philosophy in a Time of Terror* and to *Rogues*). The aporia that the notion of autoimmunity captures for Derrida is that which is at the very heart of ipseity and sovereignty. Very schematically, this means that since no self is thinkable without autoaffection, to achieve any notion of identity (and its ideal of ipseity or selfsameness) a detour through an 'other' is necessary. The 'auto' gains an affective sense of ipseity or 'oneness' through the detour of the 'hetero' or outside, so that every identity is in fact the result of an 'auto-hetero-affection'. In opening one's self up to such an other, immunity has to be dropped – hence Derrida's famous evaluation, in *Rogues*, of autoimmunity as potentially deadly but at the same time absolutely necessary:

> autoimmunity is not an absolute ill or evil. It enables an exposure to the other, to *what* and to *who* comes – which means that it must remain incalculable. Without autoimmunity, with absolute immunity, nothing would ever happen or arrive; we would no longer wait, await, or expect, no longer expect one another, or expect any event.[18]

It is thus a 'constitutive autoimmunity' that threatens vital concepts like self-identity, sovereignty, reason etc. and which makes possible and requires a continual deconstruction and reinscription, without which no real future nor democracy based on the idea of a 'sovereign (voting) self' could exist.[19]

It is therefore no coincidence that in the age of biopolitics, the political and the medical dimension of (auto-co)immunity are merging, since, as David Napier writes: 'Cultural discourse influences medicine as does medicine influence culture; our everyday notions of selfhood affect as much concepts of mortality and morbidity as concepts of health and illness affect our views on agency and autonomy'.[20]

This nexus between biopolitics and the 'medicalization' of power, and the crucial role of immunology played in this process, is also described by Donna Haraway in an important essay on 'The Biopolitics of Postmodern Bodies: Constitutions of Self in Immune System Discourse',[21] where her main object of attention is 'the potent and polymorphous object of belief, knowledge, and practice called the immune system' as 'an elaborate icon for principal systems of symbolic and material "difference" in late capitalism'. Her conclusion is that

> the immune system is a map drawn to guide recognition and misrecognition of self and other in the dialectics of Western

> biopolitics... [It] is a plan for meaningful action to construct and maintain the boundaries for what may count as self and other in the crucial realms of the normal and the pathological.[22]

From the point of view of discursive practice, the immune system for Haraway, is thus

> a historically specific terrain, where global and local politics; Nobel Prize-winning research; heteroglossic cultural productions, from popular dietary practices, feminist science fiction, religious imagery, and children's games, to photographic techniques and military strategic theory; clinical medical practice; venture capital investment strategies; world-changing developments in business and technology; and the deepest personal and collective experiences of embodiment, vulnerability, power, and mortality interact with an intensity matched perhaps only in the biopolitics of sex and reproduction.[23]

The reason to cite this long list of 'entanglements' here lies in the fact that they could almost constitute a programmatic to-do-list for the medical humanities-to-come. The discourses of immunology, in this respect, 'are potent mediators of the experiences of sickness and death for industrial and post-industrial people', while bodies, in this process, function 'as objects of knowledge' and act as 'material-semiotic nodes'.[24] As Haraway states,

> The biomedical-biotechnical body is a semiotic system, a complex meaning-producing field, for which the discourse of immunology, that is, the central biomedical discourse on recognition/misrecognition, has become a high-stakes practice in many senses.[25]

More interesting still, the more complex and 'mysterious' the workings of the immune system become, the more a notion of a body and of life more generally become entangled. As Michelle Jamieson explains: 'Today, the material fabric of life itself, our modes of intervening into life, and the socio-political, economic contexts in which these occur are thoroughly entangled such that it is impossible to speak of a natural body or biology that pre-exists our attempts to know it'.[26] It is this realization which has contributed to a return towards notions of matter, materialism and realism, especially by 'new feminist materialists' (Stacy Alaimo, Karen Barad, Vicki Kirby, Elizabeth Wilson, to name but a few), but also by speculative realists, object-oriented-ontology and posthumanist approaches.

In this context, it is Ed Cohen's work – in *A Body Worth Defending* and many other interventions – that allows for a greater understanding of how the notion of immunity as 'self-defense' has created the 'modern' notion of a body as such. However, it is also Cohen's work that provides a better knowledge of how the question of autoimmunity problematizes the notion of 'a body' and the consequences for biopolitics this might have. As Cohen explains in 'My self as an other',

> The paradoxes of autoimmunity lead us to the fundamental contradictions that underlie our understanding of what it means to be a person in our part of the world. Since the seventeenth century there has been a political presumption that "the body" is unitary and as such can serve as a ground for both human subjectivity and identity. When immunology first appeared at the end of the nineteenth century it incorporated this presumption as a natural fact, and then concealed this biopolitical incorporation by using an explicitly juridicopolitical metaphor to name the newly discovered biological phenomenon. This ideological presumption may not, however, be the most compelling way to understand the necessary intimacy of organism and environment.[27]

Alternatively, Cohen suggests that we should see 'autoimmunity not as a paradox but as paradigm [...] to glimpse the bio-politics that infects the bio-logic of immune discourse', and, ultimately, to change the entire (self-) defensive ecology that underlies this discourse, in order to bracket 'our investments in the conflicts between self and non-self and [learn] to live other-wise'.[28] Vicki Kirby's essay in this issue takes up this challenge of a 'more ecological understanding of immunity's operations' and pushes Cohen's critique of auto/immunity further by challenging the very idea of a 'sovereign self' or the existence of a 'fortress' that could initiate the immune response in the first place. The aporia of autoimmunity followed up here reaches its full prominence when Kirby combines the notion that 'neither border nor self [...] simply [are] present from the start' – i.e. Derrida's 'problematic of sovereignty' – with the emergent view in new biology and biomedicine that a body's 'auto/immune system is regulated and even made possible by "microbial activity"'.[29] This move serves as illustration, according to Kirby, that there is not only a conceptual affinity between deconstruction and autoimmunity but rather that deconstruction *is* autoimmunity at a biological level, or, as Kirby hypothesizes elsewhere, 'what if culture was really nature all along'.[30] As microbiologists Rosenberg and Zilber-Rosenberg explain:

> Interest in the "microbial" and the complex in- and cohabitation of organisms with a plethora of bacteria that are vital for immunitary functions, digestion and even behavior (cf. the notions of "microbiome" and "holobiont") have been gaining ground in biology:
>
> We are in the midst of a paradigm change in biology. Animals and plants can no longer be considered individuals, but rather, all are holobionts consisting of the host and diverse symbiotic microorganisms.[31]

And as a result, this has also added weight to the importance of new disciplines like critical animal studies, which problematize boundaries between human and nonhuman animals and instead also argue for rethinking ecologies, immunities and their self-defense mechanisms.[32]

The focus on the 'microbial' and its role for complicating views of autoimmunity is in fact a perfect illustration of the combination of changes that have led to the transformation in the theoretical landscape of the 'medical humanities' and 'posthumanities'. What carries these changes are media-technological transformation processes like computerization or digitalization. Ever since the crossover of the biological metaphor of the virus into computer language and software, the notion of contagion (and by implication the notion of autoimmunity) has become 'biodigital'. In fact, contemporary biopolitics is unthinkable without this biodigitality – or the interfacing of nature and code. It is no coincidence that parallel to the autoimmunitarian paradigm there should now be a ubiquity of contagion, as Peta Mitchell writes in *Contagious Metaphor*: 'Contagion today is everywhere – it is in the financial markets, on the streets and in our computers. It characterizes our use of social networking and the way ideas spread through society'.[33] Especially, 'new media' function according to the 'viral logic of network culture'.[34] Two contributions to this *parallax* special issue deal with this metaphorical crossover, or with 'metaphors *of* contagion' and 'metaphor *as* contagion'.[35]

Again it is no coincidence that Peta Mitchell in her contribution should return to Derrida and to what, in *Dissemination*, Derrida referred to as 'the logic of contamination and the contamination of logic'.[36] Mitchell goes on to 'map the development and evolution of Derrida's rhetoric of contamination from his increasing deployment of epidemiological tropes (contagion, virology) from the late 1980s to his shift to immunological tropes in a number of his later works in the 1990s and 2000s'. Tony Sampson's interest, on the other hand, lies in the 'virality' and 'connectivity' of media as such, and thus in the 'ubiquity of epidemiological encounters in the so-called *age of networks*'.[37] In his widely discussed *Virality*, Sampson undertakes a revaluation of the 'too much connectivity thesis' and instead further 'explore[s] new exploitable social assemblages of affective contagious encounter'.[38] In his contribution to this issue, Sampson follows up on, as he explains, 'the kind of affective encounters with desire-events [...] that contaminate the repetitive and mostly unconscious mechanical habits of the everyday',[39] and which he sees at work in (viral) social media marketing practices.

Autoimmunities – in the plural – thus illustrates the importance and vibrancy of what, extending Eugene Thacker's term,[40] might be called contemporary 'bio-media-politics', in which (human and nonhuman) bodies, as well as code and transmission processes are inextricably merged, and which constantly break through immunological defenses and create autoimmunitarian reactions and (re)assemblages. Life that is no longer clearly organic or anorganic, animal, vegetal or mineral, analogue or digital, technical or natural... clearly pro-*life*-rates and produces autoaffections and autoimmunities. Bio-media-politics under these conditions reaches its own conceptual limits. In returning to Foucault, Roberto Esposito and Timothy Campbell have been working towards an 'affirmative biopolitics' in the face of Esposito's question: 'How are we to fight the immunization of life without making it do death's work?'[41] since

> [t]he more one immunizes life, the more one calls forth death, and given that immunization accelerates in the modern and, especially, the postmodern periods, the form that this death will take will be increasingly ecological and global.[42]

Autoimmunity in the time of the 'posthuman', however, remains a vital (but also high-risk) strategy, as Vanessa Lemm explains in her introduction to Esposito's *Terms of the Political*:

> [A]utoimmunity, the radicalization of immunity to the point that an immunity is set up against what immunizes, should not be merely understood negatively, as the harbinger of autoimmune diseases that literally kill individuality. Rather, immunity should be seen [...] also as a way for the individual to open up to what is threatening to him or her in order to alleviate the grip that one's own self-protection has over the individual: as a way of protecting oneself from too much protection. It is in this other sense that autoimmunity prepares the transition from deconstruction to affirmative biopolitics.[43]

Again, the slippages between autoimmunity and immunity are telling and certainly problematize the notion that any affirmative biopolitics would be able to just 'move on' from deconstruction – a standpoint shared by Cary Wolfe. In his contribution here, he 'opens up new lines of connection between the immunological paradigm, systems theory, deconstruction and pragmatism' to address the problem of 'controlling autoimmunity' and 'political effectivity in an increasingly heterogeneous field of biopolitical actors and agents (not all of them human, of course)'.

Notes

lyrics removed from book edition

[2] Cohen, *A Body Worth Defending: Immunity, Biopolitics, and the Apotheosis of the Modern Body*, 31.

[3] Levinas, "The Trace of the Other," 346.

[4] Derrida, *Adieu – to Emmanuel Levinas*, 48-50.

[5] Ibid., 95.

[6] Porter, *The Greatest Benefit to Mankind: A Medical History of Humanity from Antiquity to the Present*, 589ff.

[7] Napier, *The Age of Immunity: Conceiving a Future in an Alienating World*, 3.
[8] Ibid.
[9] Jackson, *Allergy: The History of a Modern Malady*, 9.
[10] Napier, "Introduction," 118-21.
[11] Ibid., 118.
[12] Anderson and Mackay, *Intolerant Bodies: A Short History of Autoimmunity*, 3.
[13] Ibid., 2-3.
[14] Ibid., 6.
[15] Goffey, "Homo immunologicus: on the limits of critique," 9.
[16] Esposito, *Bios: Biopolitics and Philosophy*, 51.
[17] Cf. Campbell, *Improper Life: Technology and Biopolitics from Heidegger to Agamben*, 88.
[18] Derrida, *Rogues: Two Essays on Reason*, 152.
[19] Cf. Naas, *Derrida From Now On*, 32-33 and 124ff.
[20] Napier, "Introduction," 118.
[21] Haraway, "The Biopolitics of Postmodern Bodies: Constitutions of Self in Immune System Discourse," 203-54.
[22] Ibid., 204.
[23] Ibid., 204-5.
[24] Ibid., 208.
[25] Ibid., 211.
[26] Jamieson, "The Politics of Immunity: Reading Cohen Through Canguilhem and New Materialism," 2.
[27] Cohen, "My self as an other: on autoimmunity and 'other' paradoxes," 10.
[28] Ibid., 11.
[29] Cf. Doyle, "Allergies of Reading: DNA, Language, and the Problem of Origins," 86-108.
[30] Kirby, "Natural Conversations or What if Nature Was Really Culture All Along?" 214–236.
[31] Rosenberg and Zilber-Rosenberg, *The Hologenome Concept: Human, Animal and Plant Microbiota*, vii.
[32] See my forthcoming article on "Microbes," in Turner, Broglio and Sellbach, eds. *The Edinburgh Companion to Animal Studies* (forthcoming in 2017).
[33] Mitchell, *Contagious Metaphor*, 1.
[34] Jussi Parikka's phrase, quoted in Mitchell, *Contagious Metaphor*, 8.
[35] Mitchell, *Contagious Metaphor*, 6.
[36] Derrida, *Dissemination*, 149.
[37] Sampson, *Virality: Contagion Theory in the Age of Networks*, 1.
[38] Ibid., 3.
[39] Ibid., 12.
[40] Thacker, *Biomedia*.
[41] Esposito, quoted in Campbell, *Improper Life*, 101.
[42] Campbell, *Improper Life*, 101.
[43] Vanessa Lemm, "Introduction: Biopolitics and Community in Roberto Esposito," 6.
lyrics removed from book edition

Bibliography

Anderson Warwick and Ian R. Mackay. *Intolerant Bodies: A Short History of Autoimmunity*. Baltimore: Johns Hopkins University Press, 2014.

Campbell, Timothy. *Improper Life: Technology and Biopolitics from Heidegger to Agamben*. Minneapolis: University of Minnesota Press, 2011.

Cohen, Ed. "My self as an other: on autoimmunity and 'other' paradoxes." *Journal of Medical Ethics* 30 (2004): 7–11.

Cohen, Ed. *A Body Worth Defending: Immunity, Biopolitics, and the Apotheosis of the Modern Body*. Durham: Duke University Press, 2009.

Derrida Jacques. *Rogues: Two Essays on Reason*. Translated by Pascale-Anne Brault and Michael Naas. Stanford: Stanford University Press, 2005.

Derrida, Jacques. *Adieu – to Emmanuel Levinas*. Translated by Pascale-Anne Brault and Michael Naas. Stanford: Stanford University Press, 1999.

Derrida, Jacques. *Dissemination*. Translated by Barbara Johnson. Chicago: University of Chicago Press, 1981.

Doyle, Richard. "Allergies of Reading: DNA, Language, and the Problem of Origins." *On Beyond Living: Rhetorical Transformations of the Life Sciences*, 86–108. Stanford: Stanford University Press, 1997.

Esposito, Roberto. *Bios: Biopolitics and Philosophy*. Minneapolis: University of Minnesota Press, 2008.

Goffey, Andrew. "Homo immunologicus: on the limits of critique." *Medical Humanities* 41 (2015): 8–13.

Haraway, Donna. "The Biopolitics of Postmodern Bodies: Constitutions of Self in Immune System Discourse." In *Simians, Cyborgs, and Women: The Reinvention of Nature*, 203–54. New York: Routledge, 1991.

Herbrechter, Stefan. "Microbes." In *The Edinburgh Companion to Animal Studies*, edited by Lynn Turner, Ron Broglio and Undine Sellbach. Edinburgh: Edinburgh University Press, 2017.

Jackson, Mark. *Allergy: The History of a Modern Malady*. London: Reaktion Books, 2006.

Jamieson, Michelle. "The Politics of Immunity: Reading Cohen Through Canguilhem and New Materialism." *Body & Society* (ahead of print) 13 March 2015: 2. http://bod.sagepub.com/content/early/2015/03/25/1357034X14551843

Kirby, Vicki. "Natural Conversations or What if Nature Was Really Culture All Along?" In *Material Feminisms*, edited by Stacy Alaimo et al., 214–236. Bloomington, IN: Indiana University Press, 2008.

Lemm Vanessa. "Introduction: Biopolitics and Community in Roberto Esposito." In *Terms of the Political: Community, Immunity, Biopolitics*, by Roberto Esposito, 1–13. New York: Fordham University Press, 2013.

Levinas, Emmanuel. "The Trace of the Other." Translated by Alphonso Lingis. In *Deconstruction in Context*, edited by Mark C. Taylor, 345–359. Chicago, IL: University of Chicago Press, 1986.

Mitchell, Peta. *Contagious Metaphor*. London: Bloomsbury, 2012.

Naas, Michael. *Derrida From Now On*. New York, NY: Fordham University Press, 2008.

Napier, David. "Introduction." *Cultural Anthropology* 27, no. 1 (2012): 118–21.

Napier, David. *The Age of Immunity: Conceiving a Future in an Alienating World*. Chicago: University of Chicago Press, 2003.

Porter, Roy. *The Greatest Benefit to Mankind: A Medical History of Humanity from Antiquity to the Present*. London: Fontana Press, 1997.

Eugene, Rosenberg, and Ilana Zilber-Rosenberg. *The Hologenome Concept: Human, Animal and Plant Microbiota*. Heidelberg: Springer, 2013.

Sampson, Tony. *Virality: Contagion Theory in the Age of Networks*. Minneapolis: University of Minnesota Press, 2012.

Thacker, Eugene. *Biomedia*. Minneapolis: University of Minnesota Press, 2004.

Allergy and Autoimmunity: Rethinking the Normal and the Pathological

Michelle Jamieson

Immunological Paradox

In immunology, allergy and autoimmunity are recognised as some of the most common types of immunopathology. Both are conventionally viewed as deviations or aberrations of normal immune function, involving errors in the protective and self-regulatory mechanisms associated with tolerance and immunity. These deviations are defined by a critical mistake – namely, the misrecognition of self *as* other and thus a fundamental confusion about what is foreign and what belongs. In the case of allergy, the body mistakes foreign substances or entities (antigens) that would normally be considered harmless as harmful. As a consequence, the immune system overreacts to this benign provocation and instead of preserving the integrity of the organism, itself becomes the cause of injury.[1] Autoimmunity – literally, immunisation against self – is founded on a similarly ill-defined threat. Recognising one-self as foreign, autoimmune disease involves 'a destructive reaction of the immune system against one or another of the body's own constituents'.[2] This mutinous self-reactivity (ranging in form from multiple sclerosis to rheumatoid arthritis) embodies 'a vital paradox' as that which safeguards life is simultaneously its greatest threat.[3]

Underpinning these accounts of disease is a belief in the existence of an immunological self – the idea that the organism naturally knows its own borders and works intuitively to protect and maintain its sovereignty.[4] Immunology is famous for its conceptualisation of the body as a defended, autonomous entity entrenched in a world of invasive and hostile otherness.[5] Commonly known as the science of self-nonself discrimination,[6] it has long been governed by a thought style focused on the body's self-protective capacities, often at the expense of better understanding immune phenomena considered incommensurable with this logic.[7] This vision of an embattled self has, until fairly recently, dominated immunological discourse and the ways in which immune phenomena have been investigated, understood and experienced.[8]

Indeed, the boundedness of the immune organism has, historically, been mirrored in the discipline's own guardedness against ideas that threaten the coherence of its defended view of life.[9] Early accounts of pathological reactions privileged the ideal of self-protection as the natural referent for understanding all immune events.[10] Due to its perceived incompatibility with the logic of immunity, allergy was originally described as a 'paradoxical reaction'.[11] This view is echoed in the term anaphylaxis, used to name life-threatening allergic reactions, which means 'against protection'.[12] The force of this imperative to observe a clear separation between self and other, health and disease, is most starkly illustrated in Paul Ehrlich's concept of *horror autotoxicus*, literally the horror of self-toxicity.[13] Proposed in 1901 at the birth of immunology, Ehrlich's dictum insisted that autoimmunity could not occur because any antibodies against self would be prevented from causing injury. 'The idea of an organism incapable of self-identification in the sense that it might produce "auto-poisons"' was, at the time, inconceivable.[14]

This defence of the self has endured and been central to immunological determinations of the normal and pathological. Though the idea of an immune 'self' emerged formally in the 1940s from the work of Australian virologist Frank Macfarlane Burnet on self-tolerance, its conceptual resonances can be heard in earlier formulations of health and dysfunction in the discipline.[15] The logic of self-nonself discrimination has long supplied the basic perceptual framework for identifying what counts as disease, and specifically, in adjudicating which actions or events are regarded as expressions of a healthy organism and which must be jettisoned as alien. Thus, the coherence and integrity of the immune self rest upon its ability to recognize and eliminate foreignness: 'The study of the immune system shows that every living being knows its own identity and defends it against outside threat: [the organism] would be able to distinguish between its components and any foreign one, and would eliminate any foreign body that would penetrate it'.[16] Normal immune function, then, hinges on the correct maintenance of this distinction – that is, on the material and conceptual discretion of self from nonself.

What allergy and autoimmunity render explicit is the body's demonstrated capacity for self-reactivity – that life can harm itself. These conditions show that far from being foreign to the nature of the organism, self-injury, violence and misrecognition are innate capacities of our immune systems. Moreover, they point to the flexible and changeable nature of immune responsiveness – the volatility and dynamism of the organism's identity – which can manifest in actions that appear irreverent and contradictory. As instances of disease, allergic and autoimmune reactions belong to the broader repertoire of responses capable of being elicited in our engagements with the world. In this sense, they challenge the widely held belief that immune function is directed and regulated by a coherent immune self whose identity is given at the outset of life. Working against the phenomenon of self-tolerance – the logic that 'an organism does not react in the same way to its own elements and to those that are outside it', they call into question the related idea that self-knowledge and defence are the founding conditions of organismic identity.[17] In cases of allergy and autoimmunity, the assumed stability and identity of the self is undermined by, or centrally at issue in, the very act of self-defence – a paradox that requires us to rethink what constitutes biological selfhood.

The paradox of the autoimmune has proved fertile for articulating concepts of identity and alterity beyond the life sciences. Indeed, there is now a strong tradition in the humanities and social sciences of using immunological metaphors to explore the problem of identity in social, political and biomedical contexts.[18] In philosophy, this conversation has been dominated by the voices of Jacques Derrida and Roberto Esposito, who have employed the logics of immunity and autoimmunity to elaborate the internally confounded relation between democracy and sovereignty, in Derrida's case, and politics and life, in Esposito's case.[19]

In Derrida's writing, autoimmunity describes the internal otherness of the self to itself as the founding condition of sovereignty. Explaining that 'the worst "outside" lives with or within "me"', autoimmunity names an act of self-preservation (of any entity – be it organism, subject or state) that is simultaneously self-destructive.[20] For Derrida, this dilemma is an inescapable condition of sovereignty because no body can be absolutely immune, without an other or outside. The integrity of any body then, is both compromised and secured by an 'inevitable self-opening [...] to the other who comes'.[21] In Derrida's terms, 'an autoimmunitary process is that strange behavior where a living being, in quasi-*suicidal* fashion, "itself" works to destroy its own protection, to immunize itself *against* its "own" immunity'.[22] Here, autoimmunity speaks to the impossibility of an external referent, distinct from the self, which secures the difference between the normal and aberrant or native and foreign.

In a biomedical context, autoimmunity is figured biologically through the tropes of self-betrayal, mutiny and failure (to protect). Yet the idea of betrayal assumes the existence of something pure that is later compromised or double-crossed. By contrast, Derrida's reading of autoimmunity suggests that the nature of the self is to be betrayed – that identity is established through this founding transgression. In this sense, autoimmunity exemplifies the confounding of other-as-self as a necessary and inescapable condition of identity. From this viewpoint, the organism is as authentically and faithfully represented by its capacity for self-harm and misrecognition because this potential is what grounds identity in the first place. How might this account of the autoimmune be used to reinterpret the self-other dichotomy that underpins orthodox notions of immunopathology? How might organismic identity be refigured if we acknowledge that all responses – protective *and* detrimental – are proper (or inevitable) expressions of its nature?

Pirquet's Concept of Altered Reactivity

Remarkably, there is a concept in the history of immunology that attempted to understand all immune responses as expressions of the organism's identity, or at least, beyond the confines of distinctions between health/disease, protection/pathology: namely, allergy. It is a little known fact that the term allergy was *not* originally intended as a concept of disease, but rather as a general theory of immune responsiveness. Derived from the Greek *allos*, meaning 'other, different, strange' and *ergon*, meaning 'activity, energy, work', the word was coined by Austrian paediatrician Clemens von Pirquet in 1906 to describe the 'altered reactivity' demonstrated by an organism after multiple exposures to a single antigen or foreign entity.[23] Contra to its conventional usage in describing a specific category of pathology – namely, hypersensitivity reactions, including asthma, hay fever and eczema – allergy offered an all-encompassing account of the immune response that aimed to underline what was *common* to all reactions, protective and pathological. Against the prevailing intellectual climate, Pirquet suggested that what remained constant about, and thus most definitive of, immune reactivity was not so much the steady self-protective operations of immunity, but rather, its *mutability*. Put simply, he argued that immune responsiveness is defined by its ongoing capacity to change.

Pirquet's move away from concepts of immunity and self-protection was exemplary of the work of a small group of scientists and practitioners devoted to thinking about immune events in terms of reactivity and idiosyncrasy. Anderson and Mackay argue that this group, centred in Vienna, formed a unique thought style in immunology, especially in the early twentieth century:

> [...] we find reflective physicians and scientists with more physiological or integrative inclinations thinking about the biological complexity of human responses to disease and being concerned with idiosyncrasy and variation [...] This marginal cohort tended to interpret immune responses in terms of delicately graded reactivity and sensibility, rather than narrow specificities and facile teleology.[24]

What marked this perspective as unusual was its openness to the idea that 'the normal defensive processes of the body could become pathogenic and dysteleological'.[25] In other words, rather than understanding disease as resulting from a strict cause and effect relation between discrete, separate entities, this way of thinking accommodated the possibility that the body or immune system itself was implicated in generating pathology.

Yet what sets Pirquet's work apart from the research in this group was the fact that it questioned the normal/pathological framework in the first place. The concept of 'altered reactivity' emerged as a reaction against the medically-ingrained impulse to quarantine harmful from healthy responses, and in this sense, functioned as a *neutral* lens for viewing immune events. This fact is routinely passed over or omitted in historical accounts of allergy and Pirquet's career, which interpret this concept in light of its current definition as a specific type of immunopathology.[26] As Benedikt Huber explains:

> [Pirquet] thought of allergy in a very general sense and as a paramount term that in principle included any alterations of reactivity. Terms such as 'hypersensitivity' or 'anaphylaxis' are not the same as allergy. In Pirquet's own words, these are 'single cases of allergy' which are based on a special alteration of the reactivity in a defined 'direction'. A restriction of the allergy term on a specific direction as it is the case in its usage today doesn't do justice to the allergy term in its original sense [...] What he [Pirquet] by doing this actually made clear has not been taken up by many, which is why the problem of confusion over the term in the 'allergic' nomenclature continued and continues to exist.[27]

The concept of allergy allowed Pirquet to suspend his assumptions and observe all reactions with a naivety that he regarded as necessary and illuminating.[28] He explains: 'We might rightly use the word "allergy" [...] as a clinical conception without being prejudiced by the bacteriological, pathological or biological findings'.[29] Pirquet's frustration with the limitations of immunology's theoretical framework is clearly outlined in the short article 'Allergie' (1906), where he highlights the discipline's inability to account for changes in patient reactions observed by himself and acknowledged widely by other scientists. He explains, 'in the course of the last few years a number of facts have been collected which belong to the domain of immunology but fit poorly into its framework. They are the findings of supersensitivity in the immunized organism'.[30]

Pirquet's major problem with this framework is its dissection of the immune response into the polarized and morally invested categories of immunity and supersensitivity. Pirquet was provoked by the question of how and why vaccination (the repeated injection of foreign sera) would induce a protective response in some, and potentially life-threatening, anaphylactic reactions in others. In his article, he asserts that what is common to immunity and supersensitivity – namely, a change in reactivity – is obscured by the terms themselves. Having proven that these responses are 'most closely inter-related', he argues that 'the two terms contradict each other' and that 'their union is a forced one'.[31] For Pirquet, the incommensurability of immunity and supersensitivity suggests that these terms have become virtually synonymous with the concepts of health and disease, and to attempt to imagine them in any sense other than *opposed* seems to defy the most basic understanding of what a body *is*.

Pirquet's account of immune responsiveness as a characteristically open-ended, rather than unidirectional capacity of the organism to respond, implies a decentred, plastic self – one at odds with the monadic, defended view of the organism that, at the time, formed the basic conceptual premise of immunology as a science. In this article, I argue that the original theory of allergy finds resonance with current ecological perspectives on immune function and the challenge they pose to orthodox self-centric accounts.

Although the concepts of ecology and self or self-tolerance first emerged long after allergy, the key insights of Pirquet's work speak directly to these debates. The theory of altered reactivity presents a remarkably different and innovative conceptualization of the immune response that works to revise and transform the frame of reference, and point of departure, for immunological work. By concentrating on the mutability of reactivity, Pirquet's concept is one that emphasizes the ecological interrelationships that constitute organismic existence as *always* a complex, evolving form of co-existence. His work demonstrates a perspectival shift from the observation of specific, aggregated entities (organism and antigen) and individual organism-antigen interactions, to a view of immune responsiveness as a phenomenon expressive of a much wider and entangled ecological field. His finding that the immune response fluctuates continuously with respect to an equally changeable environment implies that the organism's existence is primarily *dialogic*, and consequently, its identity is neither fixed nor essential, but established as a lived relationality.

Focusing on Pirquet's account of the allergy hypothesis given in his article 'Allergie' (1906) and monograph *Allergy* (1911), this article explores how the concept of altered reactivity complicates a conventional reading of self and other, normality and pathology, as naturally opposed or mutually exclusive entities or states.[32] One of the more remarkable implications of Pirquet's work is its suggestion that there is no stable reference point that anchors our ability to discriminate between normal and aberrant responses. His theory suggests that the normativity of immune responsiveness is defined by aberration – a potential to change in direction and intensity. On this view, what constitutes pathology, or indeed normality, is established and transformed in the unfolding relations between organism and environment. If normal immune function is inherently changeable or errant, then there is no immutable or prior state which operates as the physiological referent from which deviation can be measured – or even understood *as* deviation in the conventional sense. Consequently, the division of normal and pathological, or health and disease, as frameworks that make immune events legible are undone by the impossibility, or mutability, of a stable, sovereign immune self.

Defining Reactivity

In 1910, Pirquet published the monograph *Allergie* in which he aimed to demonstrate that changed reactivity is a law that governs all immune responsiveness.[33] Bringing together his clinical observations and the experimental findings of other scientists, the text works methodically through a long succession of examples to illustrate the many forms that altered reactivity can take. Importantly, the monograph represents Pirquet's attempt to map altered reactivity as an object through systematic, empirical study. He writes, 'my plan is to take all the morbid entities [diseases] in which symptoms of allergy are to be found one after another, and then to collect those facts which all of them have in common'.[34] Focusing on 'serum sickness, vaccination reactions and experimental anaphylaxis in animals as paradigmatic forms of allergy',[35] the monograph outlines the scope of organismic reactivity by classifying responses into three categories: altered reactivity according to time, quantity and quality.[36] Pirquet explains, 'the change in reactivity, that is, the allergy, expresses itself in the intensity of the reaction, or quantitatively, in the kind of lesions produced, or qualitatively and in its time relations'.[37] As such, he proposes a taxonomy of possible reaction-outcomes, encompassing everything from anaphylaxis to immunity.[38]

Marking his departure from immunological orthodoxy, Pirquet opens his discussion by demonstrating that immunity constitutes an instance of allergy. As he explains, it is commonly assumed that if an individual is immune to a specific disease then reinfection with that disease agent would produce no reaction (because the individual is protected). However, using the example of cowpox, he shows that even the immune individual experiences a change in reactivity. Outlining an experiment in which two individuals are inoculated with cowpox – one who has never encountered the disease, and one inoculated with cowpox two years earlier – Pirquet writes:

> [...] both persons, after the infection with cow pox, react, the one sooner, the other later, one with a papule, the other with a pustule, one hardly noticeable, the other with considerable symptoms. The 'immune' person does not become insensible to inoculation, but the time, quality and quantity of his reaction is changed.[39]

In other words, the immune organism still responds to the infection, but the reaction has shifted in direction and intensity.

Pirquet goes on to show that the events of vaccination are paralleled by the events of supersensitivity and anaphylaxis, in that the individual's reaction to a substance is similarly altered, but takes a harmful, rather than a protective, course. Citing examples such as Charles Richet's observation of anaphylaxis and Maurice Arthus' experimental studies of local anaphylaxis, Pirquet asserts that the same process of repeated exposure to a foreign substance or micro-organism produces *both* supersensitivity and immunity.[40] Thus, each case that he documents confirms his finding: that upon second exposure to a foreign body, the organism alters its response.

The suggestion that immunity and supersensitivity, or protection and disease, are achieved via a common mechanism problematizes the nature of the difference between them, allowing Pirquet to argue that these categories of response are not physiologically or functionally discrete. For him, these response types are in fact distinct instantiations of the *same* phenomenon, namely, an undefined responsive capacity of the body. As such, allergy disrupts a conventional reading of immune function by refiguring the conceptual basis of the immune response in such a way that we are forced to re-evaluate what immunity and supersensitivity mean as both innate bodily responses, and intellectual or scientific categories. The idea that mutability is an essential characteristic of the immune response emerges as an argument against the view of these phenomena as radically different, and indeed, against the ontological and moral investment in their seemingly unambiguous, natural opposition (protection versus pathology). Moreover, Pirquet's conceptual intervention questions immunology's early investment in a rather simple notion of identity (atomic, autonomous) of any sort. One of the key philosophical implications of this theory is that it problematizes the very givenness and coherence of the organism: allergy, in its original formulation, suggests that the organism's identity is constituted moment to moment through an errant and ongoing response-ability.

The Temporality of Immune Responsiveness

One of the most innovative aspects of Pirquet's theory is its emphasis on time as a determinant factor of the outcome of organism-antigen encounters.[41] In studying the sequence of infections across which changes in reactivity occur, Pirquet was particularly interested in the role of the incubation time between these interactions in catalyzing shifts in response. Focusing on the temporal dimensions of these encounters, his studies resist the impulse to locate the cause of allergy in a discrete body – be it antigen or organism; instead, they employ an interpretive framework which suggests that immune responsiveness cannot be reduced to a simple causal interaction between pre-defined entities, self and nonself.

This viewpoint is clearly demonstrated in a series of graphs featured at the end of Pirquet's monograph.[42] These illustrations, which 'carefully [chart] specific patterns of biological reactivity', offer insight into the perceptual lens that marked Pirquet's studies as unique.[43] In these diagrams, allergy is depicted as an *extended immune event* involving a number of different immunological entities (antigen, antibody and toxic body) and a series of infections (organism-antigen encounters). Importantly, these illustrations do not represent individual reactions as stand-alone events. Rather, reactivity is portrayed as a scene of interrelationality – a processual entanglement of elements and moments that highlight the contextually-embedded and fluctuating nature of immune responsiveness. This approach, which accounts for the wider spatio-temporal context of organism-antigen encounters, suggests that no aspect is absent from, or set outside, the frame of reactivity. Here, the identity of any one reaction (its physiological outcome) is shown to be dependent on, and implicated in, prior and later reactions. Put another way, the significance and legibility of any one entity or moment is shown to be contingent on its position within a much larger frame of reference.

Pirquet's experimental framework, then, suggests an understanding of immune responsiveness as a contaminated ecological scene from which individual moments or entities cannot be simply or meaningfully disaggregated.

The emergence of time as a variable that impacts the alteration of response challenges the conventional notion of an encounter – namely, a conjunction of organism and antigen, stimulus and response, or pathogen and host. If time influences the shape of organism-antigen interactions, then it cannot be simply understood as an external context within which the meeting of these (presumably existent, pre-determined) entities occurs; rather, it is intrinsic to, and constitutive of, the way specific encounters unfold. Pirquet's work suggests that immune responsiveness is an ecologically embedded phenomenon whose emergent elements and moments are actually entangled with/in one another.

It is worth pausing here to outline exactly how Pirquet's work departs from a conventional biomedical reading of the immune response, and specifically, from the ontological assumptions about organism-environment relations that underpin this view. Owing to the legacy of self-nonself theory, immune events are typically interpreted in terms of a linear narrative of infection, in which the physical integrity of an organism is breached by the intrusion of an external, foreign element.[44] Organism and antigen are imagined as separate, isolated entities that enter into relation in the event of response. In other words, a response is interpreted as a causal interaction between bounded bodies that are perceived to be exterior to one another. Central to this account is an understanding that these biological units have fixed qualities and characteristics – that the respective identities of organisms and antigens are materially and physico-chemically given. Put simply, organisms and antigens are viewed as pre-existing their complex interrelations.

This reading of immune responsiveness exemplifies the ontology of organism-environment relations implicit in immunological accounts of disease. As Alfred Tauber argues, it reflects the discipline's 'deep-seated conceptual orientation to an individual-based biology at the expense of a more comprehensive interactive ecology'.[45] In immunology, disease is broadly conceptualized as either ontological (disease as caused by an external foreign entity, such as a microorganism) or functional (disease arising from dysfunction in normal physiological processes).[46] From the ontological perspective, commonly attributed to the rise of germ theories of disease, pathology is equated with an isolatable disease entity, such as a virus or bacteria. The discovery that specific microorganisms were coincident with certain disease states popularised the ideas of disease causation and specific etiology – that is, of disease as caused by infection with something foreign.[47] Here, pathology is imagined as a breaching of the organism's boundaries by an alien other – '"non-self" [...] is any foreign body that might penetrate [the organism]'.[48]

On the other hand, conditions of immune dysfunction identify the cause of harm in or with the organism itself. 'Pathologies of immunity', such as allergic and autoimmune diseases, occur 'when the defensive system of the body goes awry [...] when a normal process shades into abnormality or error'.[49] In these cases, disease is defined as 'a reactive and self-destructive process' – a biological fault located in the organism.[50] As Parnes explains:

> Allergy was a revolutionary concept of disease, based on the idea that damage was done not by an external agent, but by the individual itself. By a faulty, distorted, confused way of reacting to stimulants that were themselves harmless, even useful.[51]

Thus, as opposed to the actions of an infectious other, harm is caused by 'trouble from within'.[52]

At stake in these accounts of disease is the assumption that cause can be confidently located in a discrete entity – be it antigen (in cases of infectious disease) or organism (in cases of immunopathology). Both positions rest on the idea that organisms and antigens have fixed or given identities, a givenness that allows cause to be reliably attributed to one or another of these entities. Disease, then, is characterized by the containment of pathology in something clearly identifiable as other, even if that otherness resides in us. The dualism of self-nonself is assumed and maintained in the very concept of disease causality, which can only imagine the relation between organisms and antigens as an interaction or interfacing.

Yet I would argue that quite out of step with or ahead of his time, Pirquet does not assume that the identities of organism and antigen (self and other, host and pathogen) are fixed from the outset. In expanding the general frame of reference for interpreting immune events, he shows how these distinct immunological elements come to exist in relations as different or opposed, and yet biologically correlative and implicated (in specific patterns of reactivity). In studying the shifts in organism-antigen relations over time, he foregrounds the problem of how a stimulus comes to be physically provocative for an organism *in the first instance*. As such, allergy animates the question of *how* unique pairings of stimulus and response arise, and consequently, what gives any immunological element its unique identity. In doing so, it shows that the respective integrity of stimulus and response, nonself and self, is already compromised by a shared and anticipated capacity for mutual transformation.

Sensitisation and Ecological Becoming

Pirquet's investigations of allergy are essentially studies of sensitization – the physiological process by which we *become* sensitive to foreign micro-organisms and substances. Literally meaning 'to become sensitive to (something)', the term refers to the sequence of exposures of an organism to a foreign body that triggers the organism's sensitivity toward that entity. Sensitization occurs when an initial encounter with an antigen causes a very mild reaction in the organism, but a second or subsequent exposure to it produces an exaggerated and sometimes harmful response.[53] Importantly, this phenomenon animates, in the organism, a physiological awareness of its identity in relation to others – it is a process constitutive of unique moments or expressions of reactivity.

In contemporary immunology, sensitisation is the biological event typically associated with the establishment of allergies:

> There are many manifestations of hypersensitivity [...] all having in common the fact that they are initiated by an immune reaction to an antigen and occur in or on a host who has become sensitized (i.e. has previously made an immune response to that antigen) [...] hypersensitivity [...] is the result of *restimulation* with the offending antigen.[54]

It is worth noting that sensitization is a process akin to immunisation, as both initiate a shift in the organism's response to an antigen. While these processes are traditionally differentiated on the basis of whether the altered response is protective (immunizing) or pathological (sensitizing), Pirquet treats all examples of changed reactivity as instances of sensitization.

The phenomenon of sensitization deserves close consideration here because it complicates the conventional material organization and discretion of stimulus and response, organism and antigen. As mentioned earlier, orthodox accounts of normal and pathological immune function are grounded in the givenness and self-evidence of the aforementioned entities. Yet when an organism becomes sensitised to a substance, both the nature and identity of the substance shift, resulting in a different response. In other words, the foreignness of an antigen and the body's particular responsivity to it are characteristics established in an ecological relation that is constantly being negotiated.

It is in this sense that Pirquet's work grapples with the ontology of ecologies – that is, how different organisms and substances come to exist as organised systems of co-dependent or co-implicated elements. In demonstrating that the properties of stimulus and response – which we take to be materially inherent to these bodies – are characteristics that unfold through and *as* a lived relation, his work reveals the entangled and compromised conditions that actually underpin the view of organism and antigen as discrete, monadic bodies.

In his account of Pirquet's work, Benedikt Huber describes the confounded material entanglement of organism and antigen captured in the process of sensitization. He writes: 'to Pirquet the change of reactivity was dependent upon contact with an external factor [...] the external factors (foreign bodies) trigger the organism through one or several incorporations to change reactivity'.[55] Here, Huber states that the antigen is only activated *as* a trigger for the organism after going through several 'incorporations'. The metaphor of 'incorporation' suggests that in order for the antigen to become physiologically provocative for the organism, it must commune with the body of the host; there must be *inhabitation*. Put slightly differently, for the antigen to embody the property of triggering, it must first be known to that body and as such, have already provoked a response (thus establishing the conditions for future recognition). This situation suggests that the condition of the trigger's externality is its being somehow already incorporated by the host: its specific nature as foreign, other and antigenic derives from an ongoing intimacy or conversation with the host, which results from the host's directive as much as anything.

If we take these insights seriously, the characterization of the organism-antigen relation as one of incorporation or inhabitation emerges as the basic condition of immune responsiveness. If the relation of stimulus and response is an already incorporated one, then the organism cannot be separated, ontologically, from the foreign stimulus whose nature as provocative is enwoven with this body. The body's responsive capacity expresses a familiarity with, and internalization of, the other, just as the ability of the antigen to elicit a response implies prior knowledge of the organism. If sensitization tells us anything about the nature of immune responsiveness, it is that it becomes impossible to picture the stimulus-response or self-other relation as clearly beginning or ending – the idea that this relation is initiated, in any conventional sense, emerges as highly problematic. The conditions of response are such that no one component can logically precede another: the organism is always already infected, and the antigen always already incorporated.[56]

Locating the Other: How Allergy Refigures the Normal and Pathological

In this article, I have argued that Pirquet's original formulation of allergy as a general theory of immune responsiveness complicates the simple dichotomy of self versus other and its logic of a linear cause and effect relation between the discrete entities, organism and antigen. His emphasis on the alterability of reactivity suggests that there isn't a stable, pre-determined self that anchors and directs immune responsiveness, and thus, no reference point that firmly adjudicates the difference between what counts as normal or pathological. I showed that in problematizing the assumed givenness of the self, the theory of altered reactivity transforms the basic terms of reference for interpreting immune events. Pirquet's attempt to account for the wider spatio-temporal context of reactions suggests that the view of the immune response as a stand-alone event is in fact a simplification and obfuscation of the confounded ecological interrelationships that make up this unique immunological economy. This reading suggests that the identities of organism and antigen emerge and are negotiated continuously in and across moments of encounter, and are therefore only provisional. From this perspective, self and nonself are ecologically constituted: their respective integrities are given in, and yet always compromised by, this lived and evolving relationality.

Importantly, in complicating the identity of the organism as self-same, allergy demonstrates that foreignness is not inherent to an antigen, but a set of properties or characteristics established *dialogically*. This view of identity as contextually dependent is echoed by Tauber:

> From an ecological perspective, there can be no circumscribed, self-defined entity that is designated *the self* [...] Rather, the organism adjusts its own identity as it responds along a continuum of behaviors to adapt to the challenges it faces, and, indeed, 'identity' is determined by particular context. Responses are consequently not based on intrinsic foreignness, but rather on how the immune system sees an 'alien' or 'domestic' antigen in the larger context of the body's economy.[57]

This account of self and nonself as qualities that emerge from an 'economy of nature', rather than pre-determined entities, has significant implications for how we define the normal and pathological, or more accurately, what is meant in observing this distinction at all.[58] If normal immune function is defined chiefly by its openness to change, then the task of differentiating the normal from the pathological as unique, mutually exclusive states isn't straightforward. The theory of altered reactivity suggests that what grounds normality is in fact aberration. In the same way that foreignness can't be located in an entity circumscribed from the self, the diversions of immune responsiveness are equally indicative of the material and temporal entanglement of organism and environment. At stake here is the nature of alterity: understood in Pirquet's terms (and in contrast to its conventional usage), allergy evidences the confounding of inside and outside, nativity and alterity, as basic to the immune system's operation. Adrian Mackenzie explains:

> The corporeal negotiations of material differences carried by the immune system intimately determine what is properly one's body; they regulate a body open to and capable of responding to an indefinite variety of 'others' – living, non-living, [...] almost any kind of matter potentially elicits an immune system response [...] where there is no simple borderline between what is foreign and what is recognised as belonging, no simple dividing line between drug and toxin, nourishment and parasite.[59]

Thus altered reactivity challenges the primary notions of pathology in immunology – namely, an external foreign agent or 'trouble from within' – along with their shared assumption that the agency responsible for disease can be confidently confined within a specific body. Additionally, it calls for a re-reading of the conventional definitions of allergy and autoimmunity as categorical mistakes. Pirquet's novel ecological theory of allergy suggests that we might rightly interpret the instability and unpredictability of the immune response as exemplary expressions of organismic identity. Finding resonance with Derrida's reading of the autoimmune, I would argue that allergy acknowledges the body's openness to deviation as a fundamental expression of its nature. Allergy, as an 'uncommitted biological response', insists that the organism *is* a process of worlding.[60] From this perspective, difference is not a figure whose arrival wounds or interrupts a pure, prior or normative state; rather, the potential for errancy emerges as identity's departure point and founding condition.

Acknowledgement

I owe thanks to Vicki Kirby who offered guidance and support while developing this research. I am also grateful to Stefan Herbrechter for his early feedback on this material, and his encouragement to explore the relationship between the concepts of autoimmunity and allergy.

Disclosure statement

No potential conflict of interest was reported by the author.

Notes

1 Janeway et al., *Immunobiology*.
2 Mackay, "Travels and Travails," A252.
3 Cohen, "Autoimmunity and 'Other' Paradoxes," 8.
4 Tauber, *The Immune Self*.
5 Moulin, "The Defended Body" and Moulin "The Immune System."
6 Klein, *Science of Self-Nonself Discrimination*.
7 Pradeu, *Limits of the Self*.
8 A large literature exists in historical and philosophical studies of immunology dealing with the dominance of the discourse of the immunological self. These accounts include discussions of the metaphor of self, its translation into empirical research, and its relationship to alternative concepts of immune function and identity. For an in-depth analysis of the concept of the immune self, see Tauber, *The Immune Self*. For an account of how the concept of self has enabled and directed investigations of immune phenomena, see Löwy, "Immunological Construction of Self" and "Strength of Loose Concepts." For a critical account of how the concept of self has shaped the construction of the discipline's history, See Anderson et al., "Unnatural History." More recently, discussions of this discourse have shifted away from the self and toward a more ecological view of immune function; see Tauber, "Immune System and Ecology;" Pradeu, *Limits of the Self*; Ulvestad *Defending Life*. On how the conventional discourse of autoimmunity impacts the experience of living with autoimmune disease, see Cohen "Autoimmunity and 'Other' Paradoxes;" Andrews, "Autobiography of Defense."
9 For detailed accounts of how the dominance of self-nonself discourse prevented early acceptance of the concepts of allergy and autoimmunity, respectively, see Jamieson, "Imagining 'Reactivity,'" and Anderson and Mackay, *Intolerant Bodies*.
10 Silverstein, *A History of Immunology*, 214.
11 See note 10 above.
12 Kroker, "Immunity and Its Other," 273.
13 Silverstein, "Autoimmunity versus Horror Autotoxicus."
14 Pradeu , *Limits of the Self*, 52.
15 For more on Macfarlane Burnet's work on self-tolerance, see Pradeu, *Limits of the Self*, and Anderson and Mackay, *Intolerant Bodies*.
16 Pradeu, *Limits of the Self*, 6.
17 Ibid.
18 For more on the appropriation of immunological discourse in the humanities and social sciences, see Anderson, "Immunology and Philosophy" and Jamieson "The Politics of Immunity."
19 Derrida, *Autoimmunity*; Esposito, *Bios: Biopolitics and Philosophy*.
20 Derrida, *Autoimmunity*, 188.
21 Andrews, "Autoimmune Illness," 190.
22 Derrida, *Autoimmunity*, 94.
23 Jackson, *Allergy*, 27.
24 Anderson and Mackay, *Intolerant Bodies*, 36–37.
25 Ibid., 37.
26 For a detailed account of, and references relating to, the historicization or Pirquet's allergy theory, see Jamieson, 'Imagining "Reactivity."'
27 Huber, "100 Jahre Allergie," 720.
28 Ibid., 719.
29 Pirquet, "Allergy," 260.
30 Pirquet in Kay, "Allergie," 558; the term supersensitivity was originally given to hypersensitivity reactions or common allergic reactions.
31 Ibid., 559.
32 This article deals principally with his original article 'Allergie' and monograph *Allergy*. In these texts, and especially the monograph, Pirquet outlines his original investigations of altered reactivity and the

development of a scientific schema for interpreting different forms of allergy. Importantly, it is in these writings that the conceptual and philosophical issues raised by Pirquet's studies – its implications for our understanding of organismic identity and the concept of pathology – are most starkly demonstrated. For a list of other writings by Pirquet, see Huber, "100 Jahre Allergie" and Wagner, *Clemens von Pirquet*.

[33] Pirquet's monograph was originally published in German in 1910. Its English translation was published in 1911 in the journal *The Archives of Internal Medicine*. Throughout this article, I refer to the English translation.

[34] Pirquet, "Allergie," 263.

[35] Jackson, *Allergy*, 39.

[36] Pirquet "Allergie," 426.

[37] Ibid., 284-285.

[38] This classificatory approach to reactivity is summed up in the monograph's conclusion, where Pirquet organises all forms of altered reactivity in a table titled "Divisions of Allergy," which distinguishes between reactions on the basis of time, quantity and quality. Pirquet, "Allergie," 426.

[39] Pirquet, "Allergie," 260.

[40] Ibid., 261.

[41] Ibid., 268.

[42] Examples of Pirquet's graphs can be found here: http://archinte.jamanetwork.com/article.aspx?articleid=653413

[43] Jackson, *Allergy*, 39.

[44] Pradeu, *Limits of the Self*, 5.

[45] Tauber, "Immune System and Ecology," 224-225.

[46] Canguilhem, *Normal and Pathological*, 40-41.

[47] Rosenberg, "The Tyranny of Diagnosis," 242-243.

[48] Pradeu, *Limits of the Self*, 5.

[49] Anderson and Mackay, *Intolerant Bodies*, 139.

[50] Parnes, "Trouble from Within," 448.

[51] Ibid., 430.

[52] Ibid., 429.

[53] Cruse and Lewis, *Atlas of Immunology*, 347.

[54] Golub and Green, *Immunology, A Synthesis*, 598.

[55] Huber, "100 Jahre Allergie," 721.

[56] The issue of recognition goes to the heart of the problem of immunologic specificity – how the organism produces specific antibodies in response to foreign substances, or more basically, how the organism recognises foreignness. This puzzle was a central concern of early immunologist, Karl Landsteiner. Between 1917 and 1918, Landsteiner, who studied the immune response to artificial haptens (partial antigens that bind to carrier proteins), showed that the immune system could produce antibodies in response to a range of artificial or chemically altered antigens. He found that in addition to an enormous number of naturally occurring antigens, the immune system could mount specific responses to an even larger range of artificially created antigens (not existent in nature). He established that the immune system is capable of recognising substances it could not have previously encountered. As such, Landsteiner's work foregrounds the paradox that immune responsiveness is guaranteed by the fact that a first encounter has, impossibly, already taken place. For more on Landsteiner's studies of immunologic specificity, see Mazumdar *Species and Specificity* and Silverstein *A History of Immunology*.

[57] Tauber, "Immune System and Ecology," 234.

[58] Haeckel in Tauber, "Immune System and Ecology," 229.

[59] Mackenzie, "God has No Allergies," 10.

[60] Kay, "100 Years of 'Allergy,'" 556.

ORCID

Michelle Jamieson http://orcid.org/0000-0003-2333-7549

Bibliography

Anderson, Warwick. "Getting Ahead of One's Self?: The Common Culture of Immunology and Philosophy." *Isis* 105 (2014): 606–616.

Anderson, Warwick, and Ian Mackay. *Intolerant Bodies: A Short History of Autoimmunity*. Baltimore, MD: John Hopkins University Press, 2014.

Anderson, W., M. Jackson, and B. Gutmann Rosenkrantz. "Toward an Unnatural History of Immunology.'" *Journal of the History of Biology* 27 (1994): 575–594.

Andrews, Alice. "Autoimmune Illness as a Death Drive: An Autobiography of Defense." *Mosaic* 44 (2011): 189–203.

Canguilhem, Georges. *The Normal and the Pathological*. Translated by Carolyn R. Fawcett. New York, NY: Zone Books, 2007.

Carter, Codell. *The Rise of Causal Concepts of Disease: Case Histories*. Aldershot, UK: Ashgate, 2003.

Cohen, Ed. "My Self as an Other: On Autoimmunity and 'Other' Paradoxes." *Medical Humanities* 30 (2004): 7–11.

Cruse, J. M., and R. E. Lewis. *Atlas of Immunology*. Boca Raton: CRC Press, 2004.

Derrida, Jacques. "Autoimmunity: Real and Symbolic Suicides." Translated by Pascale-Anne Brault and Michael Naas. In *Philosophy in a Time of Terror: Dialogues with Jürgen Habermas and Jacques Derrida*, edited by Giovanna Borradori, 85–136. Chicago, IL: The University of Chicago Press, 2003.

Esposito, Roberto. *Bios: Biopolitics and Philosophy*. Translated by Timothy Campbell. Minneapolis, MN: Minnesota University Press, 2008.

Golub, E. S. and D. R. Green. *Immunology, A Synthesis*. Sunderland, MA: Sinauer Associates, 1991.

Haraway, Donna. "The Biopolitics of Postmodern Bodies: Determinations of Self in Immune System Discourse." *differences: A Journal of Feminist Cultural Studies* 1 (1989): 3–43.

Huber, Benedikt. "100 Jahre Allergie: Clemens von Pirquet – sein Allergiebegriff und das ihm zugrunde liegende Krankheitsverstandnis: Teil 2: Der Pirquet'sche Allergiebegriff." *Wiener Klinische Wochenschrift* 118 (2006): 718–727. Unpublished translation by Antje Kuenhast.

Jackson, Mark. *Allergy: The History of a Modern Malady*. London: Reaktion Books, 2006.

Jamieson, Michelle. "The Politics of Immunity: Reading Cohen through Canguilhem and New Materialism." *Body and Society* (2015): doi:10.1177/1357034X14551843.

Jamieson, Michelle. "Imagining 'Reactivity': Allergy Within the History of Immunology." *Studies in History and Philosophy of Biological and Biomedical Sciences* 41 (2010): 356–366.

Janeway, C. A., P. Travers, M. Walport, and M. J. Shlomchik. *Immunobiology: The Immune System in Health and Disease*. New York, NY: Garland Science, 2005.

Kay, A. B. "100 Years of 'Allergy': Can von Pirquet's Word be Rescued?" *Clinical and Experimental Allergy* 36 (2006): 555–559.

Klein, Jan. *Immunology: The Science of Self-Nonself Discrimination*. New York, NY:Wiley, 1982.

Kroker, Kenton. "Immunity and its Other: The Anaphylactic Selves of Charles Richet." *Studies in History and Philosophy of Biological and Biomedical Sciences* 30 (1999): 273–296.

Löwy, Ilana. "The Immunological Construction of Self." In *Organism and the Origins of Self*, edited by Alfred Tauber. The Netherlands: Kluwer Academic Publishers, 1991.

Löwy, Ilana. "The Strength of Loose Concepts: Boundary Concepts, Federative Strategies, Experimental, and Disciplinary Growth. 'The Case of Immunology.'" *History of Science* 30 (1992): 371–395.

Mackay, Ian. "Travels and Travails of Autoimmunity: A Historical Journey From Discovery to Rediscovery." *Autoimmunity Reviews* 9 (2001): A251–A258.

Mackenzie, Adrian. "'God has No Allergies': Immanent Ethics and the Simulacra of the Immune System." *Postmodern Culture* 6 (1996).

Martin, Emily. "Toward an Anthropology of Immunology: The Body as Nation State." *Medical Anthropology Quarterly* 4, no. 4 (1990): 410–426.

Mazumdar, P. *Species and Specificity: An Interpretation of the History of Immunology*. Cambridge: Cambridge University Press, 1995.

Moulin, A. M. "The Defended Body." In *Medicine in the Twentieth Century*, edited by R Cooter and J Pickstone, 385–398. Amsterdam: Harwood Academic Publishers, 2000.

Moulin, A. M. "The Immune System: A Key Concept for the History of Immunology." *History and Philosophy of the Life Sciences* 11 (1989): 221–236.

Parnes, Ohad. "'Trouble From Within': Allergy, Autoimmunity, and Pathology in the- First Half of the Twentieth Century." *Studies in History and Philosophy of Biologica- land Biomedical Sciences* 34 (2003): 425–454.

Pirquet, Clemens von. "Allergie." *Clinical and Experimental Allergy* 36 (1906/2006): 555–559.

Pirquet, Clemens von. "Pirquet, Clemens von." *The Archives of Internal Medicine* 7, no. 2-3 (1911): 259–288, 383–436.

Pradeu, Thomas. *The Limits of the Self: Immunology and Biological Identity*. New York, NY: Oxford University Press, 2012.

Rosenberg, Charles. "The Tyranny of Diagnosis: Specific Entities and Individual Experience." *The Milbank Quarterly* 80 (2002): 237–260.

Silverstein, Arthur. *A History of Immunology*. San Diego, CA: Academic Press Inc., 1989.

Silverstein, Arthur. "Autoimmunity Versus Horror Autotoxicus: The Struggle for Recognition." *Nature Immunology* 2 (2001): 279–281.

Tauber, A. I. *The Immune Self: Theory or Metaphor? New York*. NY: Cambridge University Press, 1994.

Tauber, A. I. "The Immune System and its Ecology." *Philosophy of Science* 75 (2008): 224–245.

Ulvestad, Elling. *Defending Life: The Nature of Host-Parasite Relations*. Dordrecht: Springer, 2007.

Wagner, Richard. *Clemens von Pirquet: His Life and Work*. Baltimore, MD: John HopkinsPress, 1968.

Self, Not-Self, Not Not-Self But Not Self, or The Knotty Paradoxes of 'Autoimmunity': A Genealogical Rumination

Ed Cohen

What indeed does man know about himself? [...] Does not nature keep secret from him most things, even about his body, e.g. the convolutions of the intestines, the quick flow of the blood currents, the intricate vibrations of the fibers, so as to banish and lock him up in proud knowledge?[1]
Friedrich Nietzsche.

Autoimmunity is a rubric currently used to comprehend 60-80 different symptomologies that effect diverse tissues and cells of the human body. By some estimates they may affect up to five percent of the populations of industrialized nations.[2] Autoimmune conditions currently include: Multiple Sclerosis, Myasthenia Gravis, Lupus Erythematosus, Type 1 Diabetes, Rheumatoid Arthritis, Alopecia, Addison's Disease, Grave's Disease, Hashimoto's Disease, Scleroderma, Ankylosing Spondylitis, Ulcerative Colitis and Guillain-Barré Syndrome, among others.[3] For the past fifty years, the prevailing bioscientific paradigm has posited that autoimmune illnesses result from an organism's deleterious immune response to its own vital matter or, as immunologists might put it, from a 'loss' or 'breech' of 'self-tolerance'. According to the paradigm's latest incarnations, autoimmune diseases seem to arise in genetically susceptible individuals when their responses to environmental challenges catalyze 'immune dysregulation'.[4] Alas, despite significant advances in characterizing the biochemical and genetic intricacies that both subtend and animate immune function, the reasons why harmful self-reactivity occurs remain mysterious.[5] Thus, even though biomedicine increasingly invokes autoimmune reactions to explain a myriad of bodily phenomena (not all of them adverse, for example the recycling of effete, dangerous or damaged cells), it does not fully understand why or how any of these phenomena exist, let alone why or how they persist as pathological conditions. Indeed, even as immunology has refined its representations of immunity's biomolecular processes to the point where lay readers might mistake them for occult texts of an esoteric religion, it still offers no consistent explanations for autoimmune pathologies.

Undoubtedly immunology now lies on the cutting edge of biotechnological exploration, in part because, beginning in the mid 1980s, the efforts to understand HIV/AIDS led to vast increases in research funding, and consequently to explosions of new immunological data. These developments generated important insights both about 'normal' immune function and about the detrimental effects of HIV upon it. They also facilitated the development of retroviral treatments now used (by those who have access to and can afford them) to regulate the precarious dynamics of sero-positivity. Concomitantly, the international underwriting of the Human Genome Project in the last decade of the twentieth century and the first decade of the twenty-first generated server farms full of digitized information that fostered increasingly dense entanglements between immunology and genomics. Nevertheless, even in light of these more and more complex biomolecular mappings, the preponderance of contemporary immunological accounts continues to rely, mutatis mutandis, on a theoretical axiom classically formulated in the late 1950s by Frank Macfarlane Burnet's Clonal Selection Theory. Following Burnet, immunology by and large takes as its shibboleth the precept that the immune system serves to discriminate 'self' from 'not-self', as Burnet robustly framed it in his seminal textbook, *Self and Not Self: Cellular Immunity, Book I*.[6]

As the negative, and 'self-destructive' corollary of this enduring immunological binary, autoimmunity conversely describes a situation that occurs when this essential bifurcation between self and not-self falters or collapses.[7] In autoimmunity, the self and its negative other somehow disregard their putative mutual exclusion, such that self instead appears to itself as both self and not-self. Autoimmune conditions thus violate the law of non-contradiction, the 'law' that since Aristotle has governed the 'rationality' of Western reason, including all its scientific manifestations. Or to put it more affirmatively, if autoimmunity constitutes an immune reaction to tissues of 'the self' itself, then it constitutes a real – and hence a vital – contradiction. In theory autoimmunity shouldn't exist, since self should not 'discriminate' from (or against) itself as non-self while remaining itself–let alone its 'self'. And although, from time to time, some of us might feel that we can no longer tolerate ourselves (or our 'selves') psychically or emotionally, within immunological thinking a self should by definition 'tolerate' itself. Indeed, immunologically speaking what makes a 'self' itself is its self-tolerance. One of immunology's first theorists, Paul Ehrlich, characterized the very possibility that an organism's self-relation could be harmful to itself as a *horror autoxicus*.[8] Yet in fact the immune self can harm itself and it does so with some regularity–and there's the rub. Autoimmunity bespeaks not just a logical but also a *bio*-logical impropriety, and as such it can also produce devastating if not deadly consequences.

Within current immune discourse, autoimmunity's paradoxicality remains irreducible. Notwithstanding the vast sums Big Pharma has spent on developing immunosuppressing drugs to address autoimmune conditions by dampening their symptoms, no treatments yet exist that can mitigate either whatever triggers autoimmune etiologies in the first place, or whatever enables them to persist thereafter. In part, this ongoing failure reveals that *autoimmunity actually names a known unknown* whose (un)knowability continues to befuddle even the best funded attempts to contain it. Indeed, the conundrum of self-mistaking-itself-as-not-self forms an impasse that has resisted every digitized, high-tech, genetically engineered means that has been thrown at it. Given the persistence of this organismic aporia, it seems there might be more to the paradox that autoimmunity 'is' than conventional bio-scientific thinking about human organisms recognizes. If by virtue of their very existence 'autoimmune' phenomena defy basic immunological dogma (i.e., self/not-self discrimination), then might we begin to wonder whether the theory adequately accounts for all the vital facts?[9] Perhaps immunology's unquestioned appropriation of a *logical* opposition – derived from and embedded in Western thought's governing epistemo-political ontology – as a *bio*-logical axiom unnecessarily limits our capacity to grasp our own complicated nature as living beings.[10] Indeed, the tensions and tendencies that the autoimmune illnesses incorporate suggest that as living beings we might not be so 'logical' after all. In which case, our paradoxical nature might ask us to consider something important, but alas immunologically obscured, about what it means to live as living (human) beings living among other living beings, both human and otherwise. At least, that is my hope.

* * *

I've been ruminating on the paradoxes of autoimmunity for a long time.[11] I first heard the word more than forty years ago, when I was thirteen. After a four-month festival of flagrant diarrhea, acute abdominal pain, and wasting, I received an autoimmune diagnosis: Crohn's disease. Living with any diagnosis catalyzes a new relation to self, but living with an autoimmune diagnosis does so in spades. Moreover, it precipitates a new relation to biomedicine. Diagnosis has defined medicine's *raison d'etre* ever since the time of Hippocrates, when medicine first anointed itself as 'medicine' to distinguish itself from its competition (magicians, root-cutters, priests, doctor-prophets, purifiers, drug vendors, etc.). Diagnosis, literally 'by way of knowledge', capitalizes medicine's investment in knowing as a therapeutic resource. Abjuring other modes of healing, medicine commits itself to knowing above all else: it takes knowing as its therapeutic trademark. Of course, there's a lot to be said for this approach. Personally, I'd probably be dead without it. But there are also some limits. For example, when my doctors tried to explain what Crohn's disease was, they said: Crohn's is an autoimmune illness. Now I had a pretty extensive vocabulary for an adolescent but autoimmunity didn't happen to be one of my words, so they tried to break it down for me. First, they said: your body is rejecting part of itself. Despite this apparently cogent explanation, I didn't seem to be getting it so they added: it's like your body is allergic to itself. Oddly, this didn't make things perfectly clear, so they threw out one more metaphor: it's like you're eating yourself alive. Ok, that I could grasp. Although to be honest, I don't think it has really been all that helpful in the long run.

In the decades since my diagnosis, I keep trying to get my head around autoimmunity. At first I was motivated mostly by a desire to figure out how to keep my gut in line, although that never really worked out. Then after I learned that my gut had a brain of its own (a.k.a., the enteric nervous system) and that the brain-in-the-gut contained most of the same neuro-receptors and made many of the same neuro-transmitters as the brain-in-the-head (including 90 per cent of the serotonin whose reuptake we now spend so much money trying to inhibit), I began to suspect something else might be going on. Taking the gut-brain axis to heart, I embraced the insights of psychoneuroimmunology: since the same peptides participate in many organismic functions that subtend our 'selves' (e.g., psychological, emotional, neurological, endocrinological and immunological) might this not suggest that 'selves' are more complicated than we usually suppose? Alas, the situation got even more muddled when, in the wake of the new metagenomic sequencing technologies, the microbiome began to figure into the picture as well, leading to the postulation of a brain-gut-microbiome axis. Needless to say, this new matrix rendered the immunological question of self even more convoluted since it might now have to include our 100,000,000,000 commensal bacteria along with our 'own' 70,000,000 cells (and that doesn't even touch on the viruses whose number is legion).[12] So what 'self' exactly gets mistaken for 'non-self' in the etiologies of autoimmune illness?[13] The paradox of autoimmunity appears to point us to a particularly perplexing problem: what if self and not-self, like subject and object, have never been quite as distinct as their immunological positing supposes? Moreover, what if living beings do not bifurcate in logical ways? And if this could be the case, why has immunology held onto its central binary so tenuously and for so long?

In order to address these questions, it helps to remember that immunity does not constitute a 'natural metaphor', and that it has not always had a biological valence. In fact, from the Roman empire until the end of the nineteenth century, immunity's primary meanings remained legal and political. Only in the 1880s did a Russian zoologist, Elie Metchnikoff, recruit the juridico-political metaphor to describe how living organisms of radically different scales comingle and coexist. Metchnikoff's innovation occurred in the context of the numerous pandemics that plagued Europe during the nineteenth century and in the wake of the subsequent emergence of microbiology (under the auspices of such luminaries as Robert Koch and Louis Pasteur) in response to these infectious events.[14] Prior to the 1860s, immunity rarely appeared in medical discussions of disease because its juridico-political valence clashed with the humoral theories that informed prevailing medical explanations. Indeed, the question of whether diseases could be contagious or not continued to provoke vociferous international disagreement well past the middle of the century. However, in the wake of cholera's repeated and deadly visitations to European cities (1830-32, 1847-49, 1853-54, 1865-66, 1873, 1884, 1892-93) a diplomatic resolution to the contagion question was hammered out at the third International Sanitary Conference, held in Constantinople in 1866, in order to settle the hotly contested issue of quarantine. As it turned out, the biological appropriation of immunity finessed the legal, political and economic problems to which the cholera gave rise, even if it left its morbid consequences entirely unchanged.

Regardless of their many substantial disagreements on the topic, all European nations concurred that cholera had 'invaded' from colonial India where it appeared endemically. (We might now call this 'colonial blow-back'). Nevertheless, given the limited understanding of how these infections propagated themselves and the conflicting stakes raised by their effects, violent international disputes prevailed about how best to circumvent these 'invasions'. Countries that had significant shipping and trade interests (especially Great Britain) insisted that cholera was only contingently contagious, primarily appearing in insalubrious locations or among insalubrious individuals, and therefore did not necessitate quarantines (which would, needless to say, impede the flow of cash and goods). Instead they argued that cholera could be addressed through 'hygienic' or 'prophylactic' means alone. Countries along the southern Mediterranean (especially Greece, Italy, France and Spain) whose ports required much shorter transit times from India and which had much smaller international trade portfolios, however, insisted that quarantines remained the only effective means of forestalling cholera's invasive propensities.

Splitting the difference, the International Sanitary conference invoked 'immunity' for the first time as a simultaneously biological, political, economic, medical and military solution. They decided that while cholera could in fact be transmitted from one person or place to another, not all people and all places were equally susceptible. Hence, places with greater susceptibility (due to hygiene, climate or other environmental factors) might warrant the imposition of quarantines; however, more favorably situated locales need not resort to such (economically) restrictive measures because they possessed natural 'resistance'. They called this resistance 'immunity':

> This immunity, as a general rule, when closely regarded, can be linked to good hygienic conditions existing in these localities, or to notable improvements which have operated there for a while. The relative immunity answers to those who are too inclined to commend the safety of nations against cholera exclusively to quarantine measures.[15]

Thus, when immunity first appeared as a biological – or actually bio-political – concept, it did so not because it explained how individual organisms respond to pathogenic challenge, but rather because its primary juridico-political valence enabled a compromise formation among medical, diplomatic, economic imperatives. If a nation was deemed 'relative[ly] immune' (in a biological sense) from cholera, then it could remain entirely immune (in a legal sense) from quarantine.

In the decade after the Constantinople conference, attempts to contain the mortal consequences of infectious diseases catalyzed the new science of bacteriology, which finally seemed to settle the contagion question once and for all. As bacteriology propelled itself into both scientific and public awareness – primarily via the labs of Pasteur and Koch – it proffered the 'germ theory of disease' as its first fruits. While the notion that germs 'cause' disease (as well as bad breath) might now seem self-evident to us, this causal relation in fact needed a bit of tweaking before it could assume the conceptual labor that it now bears. For germ theory itself contained the germ of another problem: if germs can cause disease and if they are everywhere, then why aren't we sick all the time? Or why are we even alive? Moreover, why do some people get sick when exposed to a pathogen while others do not? Since it offered compelling answers to such questions, Metchnikoff's appropriation of immunity was, needless to say, a life-saver for germ theory. Germ theory's initial limitations derived in part from the fact that Koch and Pasteur were both highly attached to – and, quite literally, invested in – the bacteria that they isolated. Consequently, they didn't have much interest in the vital processes of the organisms in which pathogenic microbes proliferated if and when they 'caused' infectious diseases. As a result, the 'fathers of bacteriology' understood infectious disease processes primarily as the direct action of bacterial agents, so that in both Pasteur's and Koch's initial hypotheses infections represented especially harmful forms of parasitism.

Metchnikoff however was a zoologist and so his main interest was not in bacteria, but in the life processes of the organisms they infected. This perspective allowed him to recognize something that the bacteriologists, and especially Koch, could not. Although Koch remains rightly renowned for his famous 'postulates', his explanation of bacterial pathogenesis relied on a questionable analogy. When Koch, a German medical and military officer, looked under his microscope at pathogenic bacteria (especially cholera, anthrax, and TB) he visualized them through the cultural lens of 'invasion' that had crystalized around cholera. Indeed, when he looked at the 'comma bacilli' that he famously defined as cholera's 'cause', he saw them as the actual vectors that enabled cholera to 'invade' Europe; therefore, *by metonymy he characterized infectious pathogenesis itself as a form of bacterial invasion*. Metchnikoff however demurred. Drawing on his previous observations that the intracellular digestion characteristic of unicellular organisms remains evolutionarily conserved in the 'phagocytes' (now called macrophages) of multicellular organisms, Metchnikoff argued that if bacteria 'invade' larger organisms this cannot be a one-sided battle, or else we'd all just be collateral damage. Instead, he conceptualized infectious disease as an inter-species struggle in which an infected organism mounts its own 'defensive' response and then, mobilizing the juridico-political term that the International Sanitary Conference settled on, he named this defensive capacity immunity. The rest is history.

However, Metchnikoff's analogy of immunity with host defence contained its own germ of a contradiction: in its original legal sense, if immunity obtains then there is no need of defence – it is literally a moot issue – and if one must mount a defence immunity does not obtain. Nevertheless, despite this conceptual contradiction, Metchnikoff's hybrid legal-political-military metaphor stuck, implicitly characterizing life as war by other means. In short order, Pasteur scooped Metchnikoff up and ensconced him in a lab at the

Institut Pasteur, the world's first for-profit bio-tech enterprise, where he worked for the rest of his life. Because his concept rectified the (il)logical germ contained in germ theory (i.e., it explained why we're not all already dead meat), the theory's proponents quickly inoculated themselves with 'immunity' as an effective conceptual vaccine. In addition to its manifest theoretical benefits, this conceptual vaccination helped to explain why the actual vaccines that they now began to market profitably worked; hence immunity justified why these new biotechnologies should be medically *and* commercially promoted. Given such tangible assets, it is of no surprise that by the mid 1890s, immunity appeared to belong to germ theory quite 'naturally'. Although Metchnikoff's emphasis on immunity as a cellular activity soon ceded pride of place to Paul Ehrlich's chemically-oriented 'side-chain' theory (the precursor for antibody-antigen models and the basis for the immunochemistry that dominated the field for the next half a century), Metchnikoff's conceptual invention 'immunity-as-defense' remained – and indeed remains – central to how bioscience has thought about immunity ever since.[16]

Fast forward fifty years. When Burnet introduced his 'clonal selection theory' in the late 1950s, incorporating 'self/not-self discrimination' as its theoretical crux, he explicitly returned to Metchnikoff's cellular position which had remained largely undeveloped.[17] Until Burnet's revival, immunology (or 'serology') was dominated by Ehrlich's emphasis on the chemical formation of antibodies and antitoxins which it envisioned as the armaments of host defence.[18] Given its non-cellular orientation, the immunochemical approach took the organism's identity as unproblematic in order to foreground its defensive capacities as immunology's proper bailiwick. Hence, its central question concerned how organisms generate such a diverse humoral arsenal that they can respond to almost any antigen they ever encounter (including synthetic molecules that never before existed, and thus whose recognition could not have been conserved through evolution). By the middle of the twentieth century, a number of competing theories about antibody formation emerged, foremost among them the antigen-template theory (antibodies formed by molding themselves to the molecular shapes of antigens), the 'modified-enzyme' theory (antibodies are 'enzymatic units' produced when antigens become engulfed in macrophages containing enzymes, which break down effete cells and other debris, that are then modified to destroy these same antigens outside the cell), and the 'natural selection' theory (an antigen acts as a 'selective carrier' that transports naturally occurring antibodies, keyed to the antigen's molecular structure, to special cells where they precipitate the mass production of 'specific antibodies' with the same antigenic keys).

The last theory, developed by Niels Jerne (who would subsequently win the Nobel prize for characterizing immune response as a function of the 'immune system') represented a point of inflection between humoral and cellular immunity. According to Jerne's theory, during embryogenesis the organism generates a vast repertoire of diverse antibodies of 'random specificities', that serve as prototypes for the post-natal production of 'specific antibodies' if and when sparked by the presence of antigens for which they have affinity.[19] However, Jerne immediately recognized a fundamental problem with his theory: if the embryo randomly generates a multitude of natural antibodies, some of them would have to correspond to molecules native to the organism itself. In order to correct this theoretical deficiency, Jerne hypothesized that antibodies to 'auto-antigens' must bind with these antigens during gestation such that these 'auto-antibodies' would 'no longer be available for reproduction'. Jerne's notion that self-reactive elements generated by the embryonic immune system are 'deleted' in thymus during embryogenesis remains central to contemporary immunological dogma (albeit now considered in terms of cells rather than antibodies).[20]

In his essay 'A Modification of Jerne's Theory of Antibody Production using the Concept of Clonal Selection', Burnet first formulated his clonal selection theory as a direct response to Jerne's hypothesis.[21] Their key point of difference concerned the manner of antibody replication. Burnet argued for a cellular origin for the mechanism (via what we now call B- and T-cells) rather than locating it in extracellular proteins as Jerne did. For Burnet, his biological (rather than chemical) hypothesis retained the advantages of Jerne's theory but overcame the objection that 'a molecule of a partially denatured antibody could stimulate a cell, into which it has been taken, to produce a series of replicas of the molecule'. Yet in framing this critique, Burnet assimilated Jerne's perspective to his own 'self' centered thesis. He cannily claimed that both he and Jerne shared the same two premises for immune function:

> The first is the absence of immunological response to 'self' constituents and the related phenomena of immunological tolerance; the second is the evidence that antibody production can continue in the absence of antigen. Some means for the recognition and differentiation of potentially antigenic components of the body from foreign organic material must be provided in any acceptable account.[22]

While Jerne himself did not employ the language of self and not-self, Burnet nevertheless lauds him for providing a 'method of recognizing self from not self'. Moreover, he extrapolates from Jerne's notion that 'auto-antibodies' are 'removed' during embryological development, to the notion that this constitutes the mechanism by which self produces immunological 'tolerance': 'Clones with unwanted reactivity can be eliminated in the late embryonic period with the concomitant development of immune tolerance'.[23] Yet Burnet's idiom is somewhat peculiar. If 'immune tolerance' refers to 'the absence of immunological response to "self" antigens' (and all 'self' is potentially antigenic), then self is defined negatively as that which does not react to itself. The choice of 'tolerance' to describe this situation underscores Burnet's curious and somewhat nebulous understanding of self as the absence of self-relation.

The word tolerance derives from the Latin translation of a Greek root (τλαω) that meant to endure or to suffer. The Latin *tolero* meant to bear, support, sustain; to continue, remain; and by transference: to support a person or a thing; to nourish, maintain; preserve by food or wealth; to sustain.[24] These etymological traces suggest that self-tolerance bespeaks a temporal process that sustains the iterations of self through time as a relation of self to itself. The immunological self remains 'the same as' itself insofar as it does not respond to itself during the course of its life.[25] It maintains itself as a self by immunologically tolerating itself. Conversely, autoimmunity corresponds to the event in which this self finds aspects of itself intolerable.[26] Consequently, Burnet found the proof of his immune pudding in the autoimmune *failure* of self-tolerance: 'It is only when things go wrong that it becomes possible to perceive that there is something in normal function which requires understanding'.[27] In other words, for Burnet, the regular existence of autoimmune pathologies demonstrated that Metchnikoff's defensive rendering of immunity essentially prefigured and corresponded to his own opposition of self and not-self.

The key issue, Burnet contended, concerns the fact that while

> [...] we were all taught to regard antibody production and other immune responses as manifestations of a process of defense against invading micro-organisms or any other type of foreign material entering the tissues [...] [t]he meaning of foreigness was something that seemed to worry nobody. Only with the recognition that there are disease conditions in which antibody is actually directed against body components–acquired haemolytic anemia, for instance–did a real sense of the importance of the body's ability to differentiate between self and not-self come into being.[28]

As the exception which proves the rule, autoimmunity emerges in Burnet's theory as evidence that immune response normally relies on a *logical and biological* bifurcation of the world into self and not self. According to Burnet – and to most immunologists after him – from an organism's point of view, a fundamental hostility must exist between what it recognizes as itself and everything else. This ontological and ontogenic perspective translates into biological terms a Hegelian proposition about consciousness, neatly summarized by Simone de Beauvoir: 'Following Hegel, we find in consciousness itself a fundamental hostility towards every other consciousness, the subject can be posed only in being opposed'.[29]

In Burnet's estimation this opposition simultaneously describes and explains the fundamental 'reason' (in the double sense of logic and motive) that underlies Metchnikoff's defensive interpretation of immunity:

> When foreign and hence potentially dangerous material enters the body–classically as an invading micro-organism–it requires it be recognized as foreign [...] Equally obviously, any body

> component must not provoke the appearance of antibody or cells which can react specifically to contact with it. Any defense force must know how to distinguish friend from enemy. The characteristic feature of what might be called the new immunology is its interest in the nature of the process by which this recognition of the difference between what is self and what is not self is mediated.[30]

Aligning the oppositions friend/enemy with self/not-self, Burnet's theory supposes that a body 'obviously' ought not to 'react specifically' to self-contact (because we're always such good friends to ourselves?). This means that self is predicated on the recognition of not-self as enemy insofar as its self-recognition (à la Hegel) must always be mediated through an other. Burnet's paradigm hence affirms 'natural' hostility as the essential condition of life (or at least of human life, which is what he's ultimately concerned with). The problem that Burnet defines as fundamental to 'the new immunology' – and which immunology has taken as its *raison d'etre* ever since – is how the organism can properly direct its hostile negativity towards the other. On this interpretation, autoimmunity constitutes a failure of defence 'intelligence' and hence manifests an instance of 'friendly fire'. If it escalates it can turn into 'a chronic immunological civil war'.[31]

The trouble with Burnet's metaphors and their ongoing legacies arises from the ways that they import certain political and philosophical assumptions to explain biological phenomena as if these assumptions are themselves 'natural'. Neither friend/enemy nor self/not-self derive from reflections on living processes; instead they issue from the way Western political philosophy has depicted how (some) humans behave towards other humans. Unfortunately, this may not adequately characterize how all organisms behave towards other organisms, especially ones of such different scales as microbes and multicellular animals. (It may also not characterize how all humans necessarily relate to other humans). Indeed, in addition to the recognition that immune function includes the clearing of an organism's effete, dangerous or damaged cells and molecules, the recent insights of microbiology concerning both the symbiotic origins of eukaryotic cells from fusions of bacterial lineages and our dependence on the commensal bacteria with which we have coevolved belie the entangled oppositions (self/not-self, friend/enemy) that have underwritten immunological thinking for more than fifty years.[32] Moreover, the persistent unknowability of why autoimmune conditions exist and persist suggests that these oppositional logics might not fully appreciate the complications entailed in being a living 'self', let alone a living being. While a few theoretically inclined immunologists have attempted to rethink aspects of this dilemma, none yet seems inclined to dispute the irreducibility of logical opposition per se as the condition of possibility for our biological existence.[33] Yet it may be the case that by inscribing oppositional logic within the vital dynamics of living organisms, immunological frameworks skew in unreasonably bifurcating ways.

Since I am not an immunologist, I'm neither capable of, nor interested in, proposing an alternative to the dominant immunological framework. However, as someone who has lived with an autoimmune diagnosis for more than forty years, I can attest that the prevailing immunological paradigm does not adequately explicate my own experience of what living with an autoimmune condition has entailed. From my vantage point, immunology's self-conception (as well as its 'self' conception) as the science of self/not-self discrimination leans on an unacknowledged and unnecessary political ontology, derived in part from its own historical emergence in the late-nineteenth century as a hybrid diplomatic solution to the economic problems of quarantine that was subsequently recruited by bioscience to supplement germ theory's contradictions. It supposes that multicellular life, and especially that of humans, incarnates hostile opposition as its condition of possibility – which means *our* condition of possibility – as living beings. Finally, by using the Greek reflexive pronoun '*autos*' (αὐτός) (which refers the action of a verb back to its subject) to modify a Latin legal concept (*immunitas*) (which it takes to mean the opposite of what its legal valence entails), immunology suggests that *auto*immunity represents the inversion of this 'natural' defensive hostility back towards the organism itself.

For me these knots of paradox that autoimmunity knits together make it less and less useful, not just to think with – to invoke Claude Levi-Strauss's idiom – but more importantly to live with. Indeed, in positing that my own cells and molecules evince a bio-molecular hostility towards my 'self' (and myself), immunological explanations of autoimmune conditions disregard the most vital thing that I have learned from living under the shadow of autoimmunity: i.e., *it's complicated*. Complicate literally and etymologically means 'to fold with'. Living beings are complicated in the sense that they are folded into the world and the world is folded into them.[34] This pleating both defines and sustains our lives. Much as immunology might want (us) to believe that self and not-self oppose one another, whether as friend and enemy or as thesis and antithesis, this framework cannot *and does not* account for the necessary intimacy that all life maintains with the world from which it arises, of which it consists, with which it coexists, and to which it inevitably returns. Francisco Varela (one of the twentieth century's great polymath thinkers of both immunology and neurology, and co-inventor with Humberto Maturana of the biological concept 'autopoesis') underscores the strictly non-logical nature of this necessity, referring to it as

> [...] the intriguing paradoxicality proper to an autonomous identity: the living system must distinguish itself from its environment, while at the same time maintaining its coupling; this linkage cannot be detached since it is against this very environment from which the organism arises [that it] comes forth.[35]

If paradoxicality obtains as the condition 'proper to an autonomous identity', then perhaps autoimmunity's perceived paradox only extends a more fundamental paradox that living itself entails. Thus, encompassing what we currently call autoimmunity – which bioscience cannot yet do – might require us to reject logical opposition as the proper basis for thinking living being and to embrace a more complicated understanding of life processes as ways of living together. In other words, perhaps what we now call biological immunity is at best an exceptional mode of biological community or conviviality.[36]

Alas this is not how immunology orients our thinking. Although my doctors were no doubt trying to help me understand what was happening to me when they told me I was eating myself alive, I now believe that 'self' was not my main problem. Instead, living with Crohn's disease has encouraged me to consider that the dynamic processes of self-formation, or what we might call individuation, remain ongoing and that they only occur in conjunction with the constitution of associated milieus or 'life worlds'. Conversely, the ongoing and creative nature of these processes opens up the possibility that we might innovate new ways to individuate and that some of these might be healing (a possibility that thinking in terms of autoimmunity unfortunately excludes). This reframing of my autoimmune diagnosis derives from the confluence between my own experiences of healing with Crohn's disease and my deep appreciation for the work of the philosopher Gilbert Simondon. By an ironic coincidence, at exactly the same moment that Burnet was promoting self/not-self as immunology's defining opposition, Simondon elaborated a non-dualistic prospect for thinking living being otherwise.[37] And, whereas Burnet's self/not-self model posits self as its point of departure and then defensively focuses on its persistence or failure to persist in terms of the negation of a negation (i.e., a proper immune response negates the negation that not-self (re)presents to the self), Simondon suggests that this positing puts the cart before the horse. Rather than begin with the individual as an already achieved – albeit vulnerable – accomplishment, Simondon suggests that we consider the relentless activity of individuation itself as the vital phenomenon.

In Simondon's view individuation unfolds from a prior condition of 'preindividuation', in which a system exists as a metastable equilibrium that contains more potential than it realizes. Given their ontological overabundance, metastable systems always tend towards change. The preindividual expresses 'a system under tension [*système tendu*], supersaturated, beyond the level of unity, not consisting only in itself, and which cannot be adequately thought by means of the principle of the excluded middle'.[38] The tensions that manifest within the preindividual pose 'problems' rather than expose contradictions, and the system then temporally resolves these problems by 'dephasing' into individual/milieu. Yet insofar as individuation always contains unrealized pre-individual potentials, all such resolutions remain only temporary and provisional, continually subject to new problematizations and new (temporary) resolutions. The dyad individual/milieu, then, does not represent a static opposition or negation, but rather establishes a 'complementarity' in which traces of the preindividual continue to resonate.

Instead of posing and opposing self and not-self as the ontological ground for living being, as immunology has since Burnet, Simondon encourages us to think 'life itself' as the 'permanent activity of individuation'. Moreover, he conceives this activity as an ongoing resolution of tensions that spur the living system to forge new connections across multiple scales of being (e.g., subatomic, molecular, cellular, anatomical, psychic, collective, spiritual, and transindividual).

> The living being resolves problems, not only by adapting itself, that is to say by modifying its relation to the milieu (as a machine would do), but by modifying itself, by inventing new internal structures, by introducing itself completely into the axiomatic of vital problems.[39]

To my mind, Simondon's notion of self-modification as a form of problem solving resonates much more deeply with what living with an autoimmune diagnosis has taught me. When I relied on autoimmunity to inform how I lived with the vicissitudes of Crohn's disease, I remained locked in a battle with myself and depended on mass quantities of (quite toxic) immunosuppressing drugs to dampen the fallout. However, once I began to allow the possibility that what I experienced *and what I am* is more than self, or not-self, or not not-self but not self, something else started to happen. Let me call this something else 'healing'.

Immunology does not encompass healing as one of its precepts, because it conflates healing with immunity. When Elie Metchnikoff forged the paradoxical concept immunity-as-defence by identifying it with the activity of phagocytes, he assimilated the notion of healing into it: 'The phagocyte therefore represents the healing power of nature'.[40] For the previous two and a half millennia, the *vis medicatrix naturae* (the healing power of nature) had nothing to do with struggle or defence. Instead it named a natural potential which medicine sought at best to enhance or support. Immunity radically changed that understanding. For those of us given autoimmune diagnoses, healing remains especially unthought. In biomedical terms, autoimmune conditions may recede, they may shift from acute to chronic (or vice versa), they may go into remission, but the propensity for self-negation remains irreducible because immunity primarily exists in order to negate not-self. However, by foregrounding the unrealized potential of the preindividual that endures through all individuations, Simondon's way of thinking living being suggests that unknown possibilities always remain. Whatever known unknowns 'autoimmunity' represents, its formulation as self-intolerance, as self-mistaking-itself-as-not-self, cannot exhaust the vital capacities that we as living beings fold into, and are folded into, as our 'selves'. Perhaps by heeding Nietzsche's admonition (cited in my epigraph), rather than remaining tangled up in our 'proud knowledge', the knotty paradoxes of autoimmunity might challenge us to consider that we are not just self or not not-self, but that in fact we are more than we know.

Disclosure statement

No potential conflict of interest was reported by the author.

Notes

[1] Nietzsche, "On Truth and Falsity."

[2] See Johnson, et al. "Epidemiology and Estimated Population Burden of Selected Autoimmune Diseases in the United States."

[3] For a basic explanation of autoimmune etiologies that includes a link to a table of diseases, syndromes and conditions considered to derive from them see http://autoimmune.pathology.jhmi.edu/whatisautoimmunity.html (accessed November 20, 2015). Recently a new parsing of the field has introduced a bifurcation of 'autoimmune' and 'autoinflammatory' diseases, the former referring to those mediated through acquired immune activity and the latter referring to those mediated through innate immune response. However, this distinction is not yet well established and it is not yet clear which diseases (if any) currently classified as autoimmune will be rechristened autoinflammatory. See for example: Kanazawa et al. "Autoimmunity versus Autoinflammation – Friend or Foe?;" Touitou. "Inheritance of autoinflammatory diseases: shifting paradigms and nomenclature;" Kastner et al. "Autoinflammatory Disease Reloaded: A Clinical Perspective;" Grateau et al. "Autoinflammatory conditions: when to suspect? How to treat?;" Masters et al. "Horror Autoinflammaticus: The Molecular Pathophysiology of Autoinflammatory Disease;" Yao and Furst. "Autoinflammatory diseases: an update of clinical and genetic aspects."

[4] While this represents the prevailing interpretation of autoimmune diseases, recently a few immunologists have begun to suggest that autoimmunity derives primarily from immune deficiencies in which the regulatory aspects of the immune system fail to limit autoreactivity, rather than primarily for excessive autoreactivity. This theory derives primarily from the evidence that deleterious autoimmune manifestations occur in those diagnosed with Primary Immune Deficiency Disorders. For examples, see: Lehman, "Autoimmunity and Immune Dysregulation in Primary Immune Deficiency Disorders;" Maggadottir and Sullivan, "The intersection of immune deficiency and autoimmunity;" Atkinson, "Immune deficiency and autoimmunity;" Bussone and Mouthon. "Autoimmune manifestations in primary immune deficiencies;" Carneiro-Sampaio and Coutinho, "Tolerance and autoimmunity: lessons at the bedside of primary immunodeficiencies;" Marks et al. "Crohn's Disease: an Immune Deficiency State;" Folwacznya et al. "Crohn's disease: an immunodeficiency?"

[5] See Tsumiyama, Miyazaki and Shiozawa, "Self-Organized Criticality Theory of Autoimmunity." 'Since 'clonal selection theory of immunity' of Burnet and subsequent molecular biological discoveries on V(D)J recombination and the diversity and individuality of immune response, how autoimmunity arises remains unclear'. For a summary of current hypotheses about autoimmune causalities see Root-Burnstein and Fairweather, "Complexities in the Relationship between Infection and Autoimmunity," 407.

[6] See Burnet, *The Clonal Selection Theory of Acquired Immunity* and *Self and not-self; cellular immunology, book one*. For a survey of the field since then see Mackay, "Autoimmunity since the 1957 clonal selection theory: a little acorn to a large oak," 67-71.

[7] Burnet, "Auto-immune Disease: 1. Modern Immunological Concepts," 645-650 and "Auto-immune Disease: 2. Pathology of Immune Response," 720-725.

[8] Ehrlich, *Studies in Immunity*:[O]ne might be justified in speaking of a "horror autotoxicus" of the organism. These contrivances are naturally of the highest importance for the existence of the individual. During the individual's life, even under physiological though especially under pathological conditions, the absorption of all material of its own body can and must occur very frequently. The formation of tissue autotoxins would therefore constitute a danger threatening the organism more frequently and much more severely than all exogenous injuries. (82-83)For a consideration of how Ehrlich's dogma gave way to the study of autoimmune disease, see Silverstein. "Horror Autotoxicus versus Autoimmunity: The Struggle for Recognition," 279-281.

[9] Indeed, classical immune theory, whether defined in terms of self/non-self, or its analogue friend/foe, gives rise to a number of regular aporia: e.g., autoimmunity, cancer, pregnancy, host versus graft disease, along with questions about why we don't develop

autoimmune responses to cells that only appear later in the life cycle (including sperm, breast milk) while we don't mount immunological responses to commensal bacteria and viruses. Matzinger offers the most robust alternative to self/non-self with her 'danger theory' which attempts to break with the immunological dogma that immunity is a form of 'self-defence', and instead suggests that immune response might better be understood in terms of an organism's attempts to negotiate dangerous situations and events. Matzinger's interventions have catalyzed a number of revisions to and defences of MacFarlane's theory. For an overview of the debates, see both the special issues in *Seminars in Immunology* 12:3 (2000) and the *Scandinavian Journal of Immunology* 54 (2001) and the special section of *Nature Immunology* 8:1 (2007); 1-13. For several other recent theoretical attempts to explain autoimmunity, see Tsumiyama et al. "Self-Organized Criticality Theory of Autoimmunity;" Irie and Ridgway, "A Modular Theory of Autoimmunity."

[10] The opposition self/other, or any other logical opposition, is neither universal nor transhistorical. Rather it emerges from the coetaneous development of political and philosophical technologies for generating "truth" in Ancient Greece as both Michel Foucualt and Jean Pierre Vernant demonstrate (see Foucault. *Leçons sur la volonté de savoir*; and Vernant, *Myth and Thought among the Greeks*). To the contrary, as Jullien illustrates, in ancient Chinese thought, logical opposition appeared as 'partial' and regarded the complementarity of contraries as a more encompassing "logic" (see Jullien, "Did Philosophers Have to Become Fixated on the Truth?").

[11] Cohen. "My Self as an Other: On Autoimmunity and 'Other' Paradoxes."

[12] The fact that commensal bacteria and viruses do not usually catalyze immune responses seems to imply that they exist in the interstices of self/not-self. In other words, that this binary is not as oppositional as its negative formulation might first suggest. Some recent hypotheses about several autoimmune illnesses suggest that the microbiome could play a significant part. See for example: Moran, Sheehan and Shanahan, "The small bowel microbiota;" Raedler and Schaub, "Immune mechanisms and development of childhood asthma;" Peng et al. "Long term effect of gut microbiota transfer on diabetes development;" Meelu et al. "Impaired innate immune function associated with fecal supernatant from Crohn's disease patients: insights into potential pathogenic role of the microbiome;" Huang, "The respiratory microbiome and innate immunity in asthma;" Van Praet, "Commensal microbiota influence systemic autoimmune responses;" among many, many others.

[13] For the best overview how immunology construes 'self', see Tauber, *Immune Self: Theory or Metaphor*.

[14] The following account summarizes my longer argument in my *A Body Worth Defending: Immunity, Biopolitics and the Apotheosis of the Modern Body*.

[15] Fauvel, *Le Choléra*, 281.

[16] Metchnikoff's focus on cellular immunity comes back into vogue in the second half of the twentieth century when visualizing technologies revealed the existence of T- and B-lymphocytes, whose role in HIV/AIDS proved so central. Today even Metchnikoff's focus on phagocytes (macrophages) appears to have been prescient, as new studies foreground the way "innate immunity" centrally participates in inflammatory processes. The best survey of immunology remains: Silverstein, *A History of Immunology*.

[17] Pololsky and Tauber, *The Generation of Diversity: Colonal Selection Theory and the Rise of Molecular Immunology*, 19-57.

[18] On the history of humoral immunology and its focus on immunochemistry, see Mazumdar, *Species and Specificity: An Interpretation of the History of Immunology*.

[19] Jerne, "The Natural-Selection Theory of Antibody Formation."

[20] The theory is currently supplemented by the notion that in neo-natal life specific T-regulatory cells are generated that inhibit autoimmune illnesses and sustain self tolerance by modulating those self-reactive T-cells that escape pre-natal deletion in the thymus.

[21] Burnet. "A Modification of Jerne's Theory of Antibody Production using the Concept of Clonal Selection."

[22] Burnet, "A Modification of Jerne's Theory," 119.

[23] Burnet, "A Modification of Jerne's Theory," 121.

[24] Lewis and Short, *A Latin Dictionary*.

[25] This aspect of the theory developed in order to account for what is now

considered acquired immune response rather than innate immune response. Today it is clear that certain aspects of the immune system (macrophages in particular) do respond to self insofar as the clear effete or damaged cells and molecules. Matzinger's danger theory evolved in part to account for this fact.

[26] In this sense, Burnet's adoption of tolerance to describe self as that which does not elicit immunological response recapitulates a classic precept of liberal political philosophy, first articulated by John Locke in the second edition of *An Essay Concerning Human Understanding* (1690). In the chapter "Of Identity and Diversity," Locke argued that the personal identity (from the Latin *identidem*: repeatedly, several times, often, now and then, at intervals, ever and anon; continually, constantly, habitually) persists through and despite diversity (which he refers to as 'constantly fleeting particles of matter'). The famous crux of Locke's thesis rests on the continuity of memory: so long as we remember ourselves as our 'selves' we remain the same person. Locke's argument primarily concerned legal and moral responsibility (he states 'person is a forensic term'), nevertheless his argument has underwritten numerous theories of the self –including Sigmund Freud's–over the past three hundred years. Not surprisingly then following the triumph of Burnet's Clonal Selection Theory, immunology foregrounded the question of 'immunological memory' as one of its key concerns.

[27] Burnet, "Auto-immune Disease: I. Modern Immunological Concepts," 645.

[28] Burnet, "Auto-immune Disease: I. Modern Immunological Concepts," 645.

[29] De Beauvoir, *The Second Sex*, xxiii.

[30] Burnet, "Auto-immune Disease: I. Modern Immunological Concepts," 645.

[31] Root-Bernstein, "Antigenic Complementarity in the Induction of Autoimmunity: A General Theory and Review," 274.

[32] Gilbert, Sapp and Tauber, "We Have Never Been Individuals."

[33] Given the increasing number of aporia that characterize the reigning immunological dogma, the paucity of immunological alternatives to the interlocking oppositions of self: not-self and friend: enemy seems surprising, not to mention the extreme hostility that these few alternatives generate among the immunologically indoctrinated. Matzinger's 'danger theory' remains the most robust of the alternative.

[34] On the philosophical significance of folding, see Deleuze. *The Fold: Leibniz and the Baroque*.

[35] Varela, "Organism: a meshwork of selfless selves," 85.

[36] "Immunity does not merely guard the body against other hostile organisms in the environment; it also mediates the body's participation in a community of 'others' that contribute to its welfare" see Gilbert, Sapp and Tauber, "We Have Never Been Individuals," 333.

[37] Simondon, *L'Individuation à la Lumière des Notions de Forme et d'Information*. This text (re)presents Simondon's 1958 dissertation, which was subsequently published in two parts. The citations used here appear in the second published volume: *L'Individuation Psychique et Collective*.

[38] Simondon, *L'Individuation à la Lumière des Notions de Forme et d'Information*, 13.

[39] Simondon, *L'Individuation à la Lumière des Notions de Forme et d'Information*, 17.

[40] Metchnikoff, "A Yeast Disease of Daphnia: A Contribution to the Theory of the Struggle of Phagocytes against Pathogens," 193.

Bibliography

Burnet, Frank MacFarlane. "A Modification of Jerne's Theory of Antibody Production using the Concept of Clonal Selection." *Australian Journal of Science*, 20:3 (1957): 67-69 (reprinted in *CA—A Cancer Journal for Clinicians*, 26:2 (1976): 119–121).

Burnet, Frank MacFarlane. "Auto-immune Disease: 1. Modern Immunological Concepts." *British Medical Journal*, 2:5153 (1959): 645–650.

Burnet, Frank MacFarlane. "Auto-immune Disease: 2. Pathology of Immune Response." *British Medical Journal*, 2: 5145 (1959): 720–725.

Burnet, Frank MacFarlane. *Self and not-self; cellular immunology, book one*. London: Cambridge University Press, 1969.
Burnet, Frank MacFarlane. *The Clonal Selection Theory of Acquired Immunity*. London: Cambridge University Press, 1959.
Bussone, Guillaume, and Luc Mouthon. "Autoimmune manifestations in primary immune deficiencies." *Autoimmunity Reviews*, 8:4 (2009): 332–6.
Carneiro-Sampaio, M., and A. Coutinho. "Tolerance and autoimmunity: lessons at the bedside of primary immunodeficiencies." *Advances in Immunology*, 95 (2007): 51–82.
Cohen, Ed. "My Self as an Other: On Autoimmunity and 'Other' Paradoxes." *Medical Humanities*, 30:1 (2004): 7–11.
Cohen, Ed. *A Body Worth Defending: Immunity, Biopolitics and the Apotheosis of the Modern Body*. Durham, NC: Duke University Press, 2009.
Beauvoir, De. S. *Simone The Second Sex*. Trans. H.M. Parshley. New York: Vintage, 1980.
Deleuze, Gilles. *The Fold: Leibniz and the Baroque*. Trans. Tom Conley. Minneapolis: University of Minnesota Press, 1992.
Ehrlich, Paul. *Studies in Immunity*. Trans. Charles Bolduan. New York: John Wiley, 1910.
Fauvel, Antoine. *Le Choléra: Étiologie et Prophylaxie, Origine, Endémicity, Transmissibilité, Propogation, Mesures d'Hygiène, Mesures de Quarantaine et measures Spéciales a Prendre en Orient Pour Prévenir de Nouvelle Invasions de Choléra en Europe*. Paris: J.-B. Ballière, 1868.
Folwacznya, Christian, et al. "Crohn's disease: an immunodeficiency?" *European Journal of Gastroenterology & Hepatology*, 15:6 (2003): 621-626.
Foucault, Michel. *Leçons sur la volonté de savoir. Cours au Collège de France, 1970–1971*. Paris: Gallimard, 2012.
Gilbert, Scott, Jan Sapp, and Alfred Tauber. "We Have Never Been Individuals." *Quarterly Review of Biology*, 87:4 (2012): 325–341.
Grateau, Gilles, et al. "Autoinflammatory conditions: when to suspect? How to treat?" *Best Practice & Research Clinical Rheumatology*, 24 (2010): 401-411.
Huang, Yvonne. "The respiratory microbiome and innate immunity in asthma." *Current Opinion in Pulmonary Medicine*, 21:1 (2015): 27–32.
Irie, Junichiro and William Ridgway. "A Modular Theory of Autoimmunity." *Keio Journal of Medicine*, 54:3 (2005): 121–6.
Jerne, Niels. "The Natural-Selection Theory of Antibody Formation." *Proceedings of the National Academy of Sciences*, 41:11 (1955): 849–857.
Johnson, Denise et al. "Epidemiology and Estimated Population Burden of Selected Autoimmune Diseases in the United States." *Clinical Immunology and Immunopathology*, 84: 3 (1997): 223–243.
Jullien, François. "Did Philosophers Have to Become Fixated on the Truth?" *Critical Inquiry*, 28:4 (2002): 803–24.
Kanazawa, Nobuo, et al. "Autoimmunity versus Autoinflammation – Friend or Foe?" *Wiener Medizinische Wochenschrift*, 164 (2014): 274–277.
Kastner, Daniel L., et al. "Autoinflammatory Disease Reloaded: A Clinical Perspective." *Cell*, 140 (March 19, 2010): 784–790.
Lehman, Heather K. "Autoimmunity and Immune Dysregulation in Primary Immune Deficiency Disorders." *Current Allergy & Asthma Reports*, 15:9 (2015): 53.
Lewis, Charlton T. and Charles Short, *A Latin Dictionary*. Available online http://www.philolog.us (accessed December 5, 2015).
Locke, John. *An Essay Concerning Human Understanding*. 2nd edition. 1690. http://www.gutenberg.org/cache/epub/10615/pg10615-images.html (accessed December 5, 2015).
Mackay, Ian. "Autoimmunity since the 1957, clonal selection theory: a little acorn to a large oak." *Immunology and Cell Biology*, 86:(2008): 67–71.
Maggadottir, Solrun M. and Kathleen E. Sullivan. "The intersection of immune deficiency and autoimmunity." *Current Opinion in Rheumatology*, 26:5 (2014): 570–578.
Marks, Daniel J. B., et al. "Crohn's Disease: an Immune Deficiency State." *Clinical Reviews of Allergy and Immunology*, 38 (2010): 20-31.
Masters, Seth L., et al. "Horror Autoinflammaticus: The Molecular Pathophysiology of Autoinflammatory Disease." *Annual Reviews in Immunology*, 27 (2009): 621–68.

Mazumdar, Pauline. *Species and Specificity: An Interpretation of the History of Immunology*. New York: Cambridge University Press, 1995.

Meelu, Parool, et al. "Impaired innate immune function associated with fecal supernatant from Crohn's disease patients: insights into potential pathogenic role of the microbiome." *Inflammatory Bowel Diseases*, 20:7 (2014): 1139-46.

Metchnikoff, Elie. "A Yeast Disease of Daphnia: A Contribution to the Theory of the Struggle of Phagocytes against Pathogens." In *Three Centuries of Microbiology*, eds. Hubert A. Lechevalier and Morris Solotorovsky, 193. New York: Dover, 1974. [The original appeared in *Archiv fuür pathologische Anatomie und Physiologie* 96 (1884): 178–93.

Moran, Carthage, Donald Sheehan, and Fergus Shanahan. "The small bowel microbiota." *Current Opinion in Gastroenterology*, 31:2 (2015): 130–6.

Peng, Jian, et al. "Long term effect of gut microbiota transfer on diabetes development." *Journal of Autoimmunity*, 53 (2014): 85-94.

Pololsky, Scott, and Alfred Tauber. *The Generation of Diversity: Colonal Selection Theory and the Rise of Molecular Immunology*. Cambridge, MA: Harvard University Press, 1997.

Prescott Atkinson, Thomas. "Immune deficiency and autoimmunity." *Current Opinion in Rheumatology*, 24:5 (2012): 515–21.

Raedler, Diana, and Bianca Schaub. "Immune mechanisms and development of childhood asthma." *The Lancet Respiratory Medicine*, 2:8 (2014): 647–56.

Root-Bernstein, Robert. "Antigenic Complementarity in the Induction of Autoimmunity: A General Theory and Review." *Autoimmunity Reviews*, 76:5 (2007): 272–277.

Root-Burnstein, Robert, and De Kisa Fairweather. "Complexities in the Relationship between Infection and Autoimmunity." *Current Allergy and Asthma Report*, 14 (2014): 407.

Silverstein, Arthur. "Horror Autotoxicus versus Autoimmunity: The Struggle for Recognition." *Nature Immunology*, 2:4 (2001): 279–281.

Silverstein, Arthur. *A History of Immunology*. San Diego, Calif.: Academic Press, 1989.

Simondon, Gilbert. *L'Individuation à la Lumière des Notions de Forme et d'Information*. Grenoble: Èditions Jérome Millon, 2005.

Simondon, Gilbert. *L'Individuation Psychique et Collective*. Paris: Aubrier, 1989.

Tauber, Alfred. *Immune Self: Theory or Metaphor*. New York and Cambridge: Cambridge University Press, 1994.

Touitou, Isabelle. "Inheritance of autoinflammatory diseases: shifting paradigms and nomenclature." *Journal of Medical Genetics*, 50 (2013): 349–359.

Tsumiyama, K., Y. Miyazaki, and S. Shiozawa (2009) "Self-Organized Criticality Theory of Autoimmunity." *PLoS ONE*, 4:12 (2009): e8382.

Van Praet, Jens. "Commensal microbiota influence systemic autoimmune responses." *EMBO Journal*, 34:4 (2015): 466–74.

Varela, Francisco. "Organism: a meshwork of selfless selves." In *Organism and the origins of self*, edited by A Tauber, 79–107. Boston: Kluwer Academic Publishers, 1991.

Vernant, Jean-Pierre. *Myth and Thought among the Greeks*. Trans. Janet Lloyd and Je Fort. New York: Zone, 2006.

Yao, Q. and D. E. Furst. "Autoinflammatory diseases: an update of clinical and genetic aspects." *Rheumatology*, 47 (2008): 946–951.

Autoimmunity: the political state of nature

Vicki Kirby

A centipede was happy – quite!
Until a toad in fun
Said, 'Pray, which leg moves after which?'
This raised her doubts to such a pitch,
She fell exhausted in the ditch
Not knowing how to run.
Katherine Craster, 'The Centipede's Dilemma'.[1]

A feeling of apprehension accompanies the word 'immunity' because it reminds us that our sense of being, of being able and well, is under constant threat. We have all seen computerised animations of those internal battles where armies of phagocytic cells and their squads of macrophages, neutrophils, granulocytes and other specialist crack teams are mobilised against an invading pathogen. The orchestration of the attack seems as wonderful as it is mysterious, especially as this first, spontaneous response is subsequently supported by a battery of more considered stratagems. The latter take time – days, or even a week – because antigen specific defence mechanisms must consult libraries of historical records as part of their intelligence gathering. These military metaphors seem especially apt as we imagine the moves and counter moves of a battlefield: there is a war going on! And so we cling to the hope that our immune system's silent skirmishes will prevail against sickness and decline, against being undone, against feeling unsure of who we are. However, this tale of routing the enemy is far from accurate, especially when we consider the riddle of autoimmunity.[2] As we broaden our understanding of how immunity works, or why the very notion of immunity is problematic, combative and plague metaphors lose much of their explanatory relevance. Indeed, as we begin to appreciate the labyrinthine nature of what autoimmunity involves and the way the phenomenon touches every aspect of our lives, things get crazy.

The aim of this meditation is to explore, in a preliminary way, some of the reasons why autoimmunity might give us pause. I plan to dip into arguments that specifically address the immune system and the social and political implications of its representation. Yet these particular literatures are not central to the overall direction I want to take.[3] Although my own interest in autoimmunity will be introduced through its biological implications, it is the larger question of identity and selfhood – *autos*, *ipse* – regardless of disciplinary or discursive context and the specifics of subject matter, which especially interests me. For this reason I prefer to begin gently with a more personal point of entry into what can only be described as autoimmunity's confounding riddle.

Many of us are painfully aware that a significant percentage of the population suffers from an autoimmune disease. As I type this text my increasingly deformed fingers certainly place me in this category. Heberden's nodes are the bony and painful swellings of osteoarthritis that appear at finger joints, usually those closest to the nail, which twist the fingers into misshapen and almost comical appearance.[4] I say comical because a friend and I have found the comparison of our respective digital malformations quite hilarious. But perhaps the reason for the laughter isn't straightforward. The hand is extended out towards the other and evaluated – the state of the nails, nail bed and quick, or the general appearance of the back of the hand, age spots, hairiness, size and shape of the fingers, smooth or calloused palms, sweaty or dry skin, the differential pressure in the grasp of a hand-shake,[5] racial and gender markers – the metrics of judgement are swift and often unforgiving.

Hands are read as signs of many things, including character, and the indignity of unruly fingers can be felt as a personal betrayal. However, as with all readings, interpretations can be as errant and unpredictable as these delinquent fingers. I keenly recall an image of Cathleen Nesbitt, an English actress who played the part of Cary Grant's grandmother in the film, *An Affair to Remember* (1957). Her hands may have been deformed by rheumatoid arthritis, a much more painful and debilitating autoimmune disease that can bend the entire hand or individual fingers in a more horizontal direction to the forearm and leave the sufferer effectively crippled. I remember that Nesbitt was playing the piano a little hesitantly, which only added to the intended picture of benign wisdom, stoical perseverance and self-sufficiency. She wore a rather large ring or rings on her wedding finger – interestingly, in my memory she wore many rings on many fingers – and the overall effect was, quite simply, attractive. There was a message in her hands that trumped the mercurial adjudications of beauty. 'I will persist against the odds. Here is proof that I can survive all that life throws at me! Look!' And yet it is precisely this rather comforting image of a self, triumphant in the face of life's capricious lottery of pain and suffering, that brings into question the riddle of autoimmunity. It is the very nature of the self as an identifiably enduring entity – defended against alien assault and willing itself forward – that now proves elusive. The reason for this is strangely perverse, because although not consciously invited, the pain and suffering could be described as self-inflicted. And yet this description is misleading and its terms feel decidedly wrong because they are morally charged with blame: you did this to yourself! Nevertheless, what is at stake in this confusion of external with internal and cause with effect is the very status of the 'self' that anchors the description and its various qualifications and correctives. Put simply, what is the nature of this self that can have no identificatory kernel to anchor its mutations, no point of reference that discovers the site of agency and unequivocal intention?

As we have seen, immunity appears in the form of a defended self, actively deploying security forces against unwelcome infiltration. However, *auto*immunity suggests that this sovereign self is strangely duplicitous and even suicidal. We might have thought that the vigilance against what is foreign and potentially harmful is intended to preserve and indemnify the self, and yet this 'defending' force can target the body's own tissues in an act of apparent misrecognition. The legible trace of many autoimmune diseases can even be seen in ancient skeletons, such as the arthritic vertebrae of aboriginal 'Mungo Man' who lived 40,000-60,000 years ago. And yet, despite evidence of such a long history, the actual phenomenon of autoimmunity wasn't properly acknowledged until around the middle of last century, and even then it came about after several false starts and for serendipitous reasons.[6] In his magnum opus, *A Body Worth Defending*, Ed Cohen tracks the ways in which this notion of defence is retained despite the growing awareness of autoimmunity's foundational quandary. MacFarlane Burnett, for example, argues for a self/non-self dichotomy as an explanatory distinction in 1969,[7] and the editors of a journal issue on contemporary immune theories reinforce the preferability of this account as recently as 2000: 'Everyone agrees that a biodestructive defense mechanism must make some kind of self-nonself discrimination'.[8] However, Cohen remains unconvinced by this 'lexical transition' that repeats some version of agonism as its unquestioned default line. As he explains the problem, 'the analogy "self is to non-self as friend is to foe" reveals the immunological self-relation as decisively *political*'.[9] Importantly for Cohen, the assumption that politics and biology can be confused, even conflated in this way, should give us pause.

And so we reach the real dilemma with this subject matter, namely, how to describe the phenomenon of autoimmunity in a way that will effectively acknowledge its intrinsic conundrum. In the main, I agree with Cohen's observations and appreciate his concern with the way that social decisions are naturalised in order to make broader political agendas appear prescribed and incontestable. However, I should note in anticipation of my argument's direction that an inevitable defensiveness in Cohen's own position will force him to commit to something, unwittingly it would seem, that I want to contest. To briefly explain this subtle yet important disagreement, Cohen determines that the flaw in the logic of immunity is its inaugural appeal to a defended self. In this we are in agreement, for there is no real evidence that a fortress self initiates the immune response or, more profoundly – and this, for me, is the sticking point – there is no real evidence that a sovereign self that might with time succumb to outside, or even, internal forces, ever existed. Interestingly however, Cohen's disquiet is less with immunity's particular foundational departure point than with the danger of such representations when they appear 'as intrinsic to the individual organism, projecting [the model's] politics into the living being as a vital condition [...] push[ing] it even deeper into the organism, to the level of ontogeny if not ontology'.[10]

And yet it could be argued that Cohen's fear of this slide into naturalisation says more about the dangers of assuming that biology/nature is, indeed, the programmatic, static and unthinking support of an agential mind that is uniquely placed to practice the politics of misrepresentation. What I hope to suggest in this meditation is why Cohen's argument against the equation of nature with prescriptive determination might be furthered rather than hindered if we appreciate that nature *is* intrinsically, ontologically, political. Ironically, Cohen's objection to a sovereign self (mind) who requires defending against an outside is inadvertently recuperated in the prohibitive proposition that political representations are not generated naturally. It seems that both nature and culture are sovereign entities in this account, hermetically enclosed and successfully immune to each other's internal machinations![11]

To return to the image of 'a self defended' and to unpack why this representation is much too simplistic, Cohen refers us to the immunologist, Polly Matzinger, who also objects to the 'Cold War' imagery that attends immunity discourse. Preferring what we might call a more ecological understanding of immunity's operations, Matzinger perceives the self as 'a habitat, welcoming the presence of useful commensal organisms and allowing the passage of harmless, opportunistic ones. With such an immune system we live in harmony with our external and internal environment'.[12] Importantly, by replacing the self/other image of a militarised border crossing, focussed on danger and threat, with one that can accommodate a foreign other where this seems warranted, or even reject aspects of the self for the same reasons, Matzinger is able to refuse the negative implications of bellicose metaphors and offer a more pacific solution. This concern with the political appropriateness of medical descriptions and their social consequences, something we have already seen in Cohen's intervention, is salutary, and my own argument is not intended to denigrate the value of these analyses. Nevertheless and despite this, the problematic we are investigating is so convoluted and perverse in its ontological implications that it exceeds the logic of error versus corrective that motors these well-intended interventions.

To dilate briefly on this last point, the appeal of the corrective echoes the theological imperative to segregate good from bad, or right from wrong, and even secular debate is moulded in these same terms. The fact is that most of us find these either/or discriminations compelling, positing a prelapsarian integrity and relative purity before the fall into corruption and error, or its inverse, we tend to defend what we deem as progress and complexity against an original simplicity, naiveté or ignorance. Either way we seem driven to take sides and to promote a notion of benefit in the form of forward progress or nostalgic return: we may choose to offer remedial insights or we may defend against a particular correction. However, such is the inescapable and perverse nature of this mirror logic that even if we could choose to do nothing, to decline this one-or-other two-step, then inasmuch as we perceive our position as different from the latter we reiterate the same binary logic in the very act of refusing it. The point of this small detour is to suggest that a discussion of autoimmunity cannot be inoculated against this same sticky ambiguity and confusion: one thing can very quickly appear as its opposite when our analysis equates difference with the separations of b/ordering.

As we have seen, the autonomy of a self, or more profoundly, the very notion that there is a self whose integrity can be menaced and compromised from without, becomes the moral default line for the immunity model and its border police. However, the suggestion that the border is significantly porous and that welcoming what is apparently alien can facilitate ecological harmony, or that danger may well be self-generated and already present within the organism – these concessions appear to complicate, if not entirely overturn, the immunity model's brutal intolerance. But has the former's more permissive perspective effectively displaced the question of self and other (Cohen's friend versus foe) rather than addressing what it is that is tolerating or defending? 'Who' or 'what' is making these discriminations, for better and/or for worse? It seems fair to ask, for example, why an appeal to ecology should appear intrinsically harmonious when life's operations must embrace all those behaviours and temperaments whose strategic opportunisms might appear otherwise. If life is lived adaptively – a perpetual motion machine – and if change is constant and volatility clearly in evidence, then what can 'harmony' actually mean? We might think of the well-worn phrase, 'Nature, red in tooth and claw' from the poem, 'In Memoriam A.H.H.' by Alfred Lord Tennyson on the death of his friend. Its sentiment is routinely deployed as a fair description of Charles Darwin's apparent abandonment of God, and further, of his assault on an original state of Nature (Eden) as one of benign accord. As recently as 1976, Roger Penrose famously deployed the phrase again as a summation of his own conviction. 'I think "nature red in tooth and claw" sums up our modern understanding of natural selection admirably' (1976, 2). In these times where local versus global is an increasingly qualified and contested distinction because what is deemed to be outside a particular ecology is, from another perspective, just more imbricated ecology – can we comfortably accept that any entity is straightforwardly autonomous and circumscribed, or definitively harmless? Or here, can the turn to porosity complicate the sense of a border or self to such an extent that we can concede the wonder and terror of autoimmunity, where neither border nor self is simply present *from the start*?

In sum, autoimmunity's riddle must accommodate the following paradox: the concept of *autos*, or *ipse* can no longer be some*thing* which is compromised, threatened or even secured, and this is because an identifiable self which appears under attack may never have existed. Given this apparent madness we begin to see why a robust discussion of autoimmunity as some-*thing* unusual and presumably identifiable must also succumb to this same suicidal logic. Clearly, we will need to proceed slowly if we are to proceed at all! To return to Matzinger's account, she succeeds in redirecting the conversation when she begins with a compromised self that falls prey to its own dangerous duplicities. Nevertheless, and this is the problem, this description of self-deception must posit a true self that can recognise its fraudulent doppelgänger and move against this 'dangerous' impostor. Or to put this another way, and as noted previously when we used the term misrecognition to describe autoimmunity as a failure of sorts, it is a sovereign self who can recognise and be recognised that makes this description operationally useful. However, rather than mount critique after critique – an infinite regress of failed representations – perhaps a different perspective might harness aspects of this insight for another reading. If we entertain the suggestion, however difficult, that autoimmunity places the self (*ipse, autos*) under erasure, in other words, if this is not simply a suicidal agonism or self divided because there is no self that will anchor such descriptions, then the status of all evaluative terms, whether danger, wellness or benefit, would prove equally problematic. In other words, what foundational reference point can securely anchor these judgements? Or to put this another way, how is the difference between advantage and threat determined and by 'whom'?[13]

Importantly, when Matzinger contests the view that the body is made vulnerable at the site of a self/non-self border crossing, she does more than choose a more benign explanation of encounter. She effectively rejects the notion of a sovereign self whose integrity is at risk, a sovereign self that can have any borders at all! And yet this self whose identity is undone on the one hand is inevitably reintroduced on the other. As positives such as self and integrity, harmony and ecology, or negatives such as danger, threat and disequilibrium, all prove incapable of bearing the explanatory weight that these descriptions presume; a metonymy of supporting terms works to buttress their credibility and to prevent further interrogation of what, exactly, constitutes the departure point for these discussions. For example, when we attribute an immune system with the cognitive capacity to recognise danger and have sufficient forethought to mount an effective response we install an imminent cogito, a discriminating self that is sufficiently aware of its own interests to monitor what is required to maintain wellbeing. Interestingly, this cogito must appear *as* biology. On the one hand, to imagine biology as inherently agential and cognising would allow us to attribute 'meat' with discriminating powers and behaviours, wherein adjectives such as bellicose, tolerant or even pacifist might not be inappropriate. However, an added and more awkward implication is that the biological self would also be capable of folly and inattention, behaviours whose consequences may well prove harmful and self-undermining. But regardless of these different possibilities, the convention in cultural analysis is to describe such readings as mistaken projections, the ruse of anthropocentric metaphors that confuse politics (culture) with nature. Indeed, we saw this very assumption in Cohen's earlier warning. Given the recognised discomfort with arguments that attribute biology with intention our question becomes, where does agency properly reside? It seems that the problematic of sovereignty can't be explored without already assuming what is in question, because if we reject an imminent, biological self our tendency is to surreptitiously upload the required capacities into a transcendental self, where intention arrives like a *deus ex machina* that requires no further explanation.

Autoimmunity's status takes us into a confusing maze of questions from which there is no straightforward exit or solution. However, rather than interpret this labyrinth of possibilities in terms of an impending loss or hopeful rediscovery of self – as if the question about a sovereign self can be answered, finally, in either the affirmative or the negative – we can instead use this disorientation as an opportunity to reconsider the analytical terms that inform such discussions. If this hesitant forward movement lacks a clear sense of progress, by dint of this very uncertainty we are at least afforded the chance to revisit our initial assumptions about identity as such. With this as our aim a review of Matzinger's specific objections to the self/other immunity model alerts us to some interesting anomalies. The integrity and autonomy of the subject has long been complicated by replacing continuity with discontinuity, or a sense of the whole with a jigsaw of parts or fragments, as we see in the cyborg, or hybrid self. Matzinger's sense of danger has already evoked such an image of a living amalgamation, an ecology of entities both within and without. However, Matzinger underlines the quandary of selfhood with further examples whose logics, when taken together, make no apparent sense. Cohen summarises some of the oddities already acknowledged by Matzinger herself, for which

> defense-oriented immunology cannot account, including, among others, autoimmunity [...] why tumours are not rejected; why mothers do not reject foetuses; why we can go through puberty, maternity and aging without rejecting ourselves; why we do not defend against commensal bacteria and viruses (e.g., the bacteria in our guts without which we are dead meat).[14]

The truth of Cohen's assertion that without the microbiome to facilitate digestion, health and survival we are 'dead meat' is reasonably well known, and interestingly, this image again evokes a cyborgian understanding of self. Such representations of indebtedness posit a self and a supplement, a self whose very being requires an additional bacterial ecology in order to further its survival chances. And yet as we have seen in previous examples things get murky if we investigate our initial assumptions about what it is that pre-exists and is enhanced, or sometimes disadvantaged, by this parasitic support. If we break this down into its most basic building blocks we could say that the sense of self, especially what constitutes a specifically human self, will involve such capacities as cognition, memory, personality and mood – the very signature of human exceptionalism. It goes without saying that the human biome isn't itself human; rather, it is a micro-environment of tiny creatures that enable and promote what is *already* human. However, what is truly astonishing about the ontological difference between this biome and the specificity of our being is perhaps nothing at all if we consider this question in light of recent scientific findings. Kathy Magnusson, for example, is principal researcher with the Linus Pauling Institute and her team's research on gut microflora appeared in a recent issue of *Neuroscience*.[15] Explaining the significance of these results for a lay audience in *Neuroscience News*, she explains why the human biome is integral to 'cognitive flexibility':

> Bacteria can release compounds that act as neurotransmitters, stimulate sensory nerves or the immune system, and affect a wide range of biological functions. We're not sure just what messages are being sent, but we are tracking down the pathways and the effects.[16]

The role of the Enteric System (ENS) in cognition,[17] as well as the involvement of bacterial 'passengers' in determining what we conventionally call agency, behaviour, cognition and temperament, certainly complicate the mind/body division, and in ways that are bewildering to contemplate. In effect we are forced to confront the suggestion that the corporeal residence of an individual – the site of self or ego – includes the bowel, and further, that this ego – this most intimate sense of personal identity – may well 'be' an intra-species agent that confounds the human/non-human opposition altogether. Titles in popular science journals in this relatively new research area point us in these provocative directions. In an article by Robert Martone in *Scientific American* we read, 'The Neuroscience of the Gut - *Strange but true: the brain is shaped by bacteria in the digestive tract*',[18] and in a report in *New Scientist* by Emma Young – 'Gut instincts: The secrets of your second brain', we learn that 'when it comes to your moods, decisions and behavior, the brain in your head is not the only one doing the thinking'.[19]

An accessible summation of why such research represents an assault on sovereign identity, even embracing the broader question of how the identity of human species being might be corralled against its others, appeared in a recent issue of the *The New York Times* under the header, 'Can the Bacteria in Your Gut Explain Your Mood?'. I cite a small excerpt of Peter Andrey Smith's article because it helps to illuminate why the problematic of autoimmunity is poorly understood when its riddle is reduced to the logic of the supplement, that is, to one plus one, or indeed, one plus many (others), as we witness in the image of the hybrid or cyborg entity. What concerns us here is the initial investment in a foundational entity whose apparent unity and integrity is existentially precedent to what will later befall or enhance its fortunes.

> Biologists now believe that much of what makes us human depends on microbial activity. The two million unique bacterial genes found in each human microbiome can make the 23,000 genes in our cells seem paltry, almost negligible, by comparison. 'It has enormous implications for the sense of self', Tom Insel, the director of the National Institute of Mental Health, told me. 'We are, at least from the standpoint of DNA, more microbial than human. That's a phenomenal insight and one that we have to take seriously when we think about human development.' [20]

Insel's statement that the DNA in microbial flora literally outweighs our human DNA is certainly fascinating in itself, but the point at issue can remain invisible when these comparisons begin with component parts that are later aggregated. For example, Mark Lyte, another prominent researcher in this field and mentioned in the same article, attributes microbiota with explanatory relevance regarding behaviour – *our* behaviour. Yet again, by sticking to the cause/effect logic of interference – microbiota 'influence' our behaviour – Lyte can secure the difference between human identity and its others while at the same time calling into question what makes us human in the first instance. It seems reasonable to wonder what human behaviour might be *without* gut flora. As we saw above, Ed Cohen suggested that without gut bacteria 'we are dead meat'. The conventional reading that a much needed prop will aid survival, however, takes on quite a different hue if our psychological and behavioural identity is inherently bacterial. With reference to experiments in primate behaviour, Lyte provocatively argues that, 'if you transfer the microbiota from one animal to another, you can transfer the behaviour'.[21] We would need to explore the terms of this claim further, inasmuch as the very notion of a discrete behaviour reinstalls this notion of an identifiable 'something' that transcends species context, thereby rendering the notion of a substantive referent, a departure point, a unit of exchange, as some*thing* we needn't question. Nevertheless, it seems reasonable to wonder how agency can be dispersed across species and still be described as properly 'mine'.[22]

If the very essence of human *ipseity* and the *autos* is under erasure, such that it isn't clear how 'it' can 'possess' an immune or an autoimmune system (because both terms already assume what is now in question), we are left to wonder how a robust discussion of sovereignty can proceed at all. Importantly, this difficulty is not restricted to biological concerns, for as Michael Naas describes the general consequences of this phenomenon,

> 'autoimmunity' appears to name a process that is inevitably and irreducibly at work more or less everywhere, at the heart of every sovereign identity. Not simply a method or strategy of reading, 'autoimmunity' [...] comes to affect not only the bodies we call discourses and texts but psychic systems and political institutions, nation-states and national contexts, and perhaps even, though this is the most contentious, God himself, God in his sovereign self, or in his phantasmatic, theologico-political body.[23]

Naas's discussion is especially indebted to Jacques Derrida's essay, *Rogues*, where the term 'autoimmunity' is deployed in a way that resonates with his use of other neologisms, such as 'supplementarity' or '*différance*', terms (or non-concepts) that defy precise definition because unravelling their meanings and implications involves a knotty tangle of related associations that proves endless. Another of Derrida's neologisms, '*destinerrance*', also evokes this sense that we never quite arrive at our goal, or similarly, that our departure point will prove equally elusive and difficult to pinpoint. Such images might evoke the figures of Sisyphus, or Tantalus, whose behaviours remain goal-oriented; the former strives to push his stone to the very top of the hill and the latter perseveres in trying to quench his thirst and satisfy his hunger – all to no avail. I mention these examples because within cultural analysis of various stripes there is a tendency to understand the problematic of origin, goal or outcome – and identity more generally – in terms of failure. The tendency is to posit an entity whose borders have been breached and integrity undone. Or we theorise a self who succumbs to the alien within; a self who can't reach a goal or retrieve a now lost and therefore inaccessible origin; a self whose consciousness (ego) is rudely ambushed by an unconscious that waylays an original intention, and so on. My own view is that readers of deconstruction can remain wedded to this style of logic that installs identity as its foundational commitment only to then acknowledge a failure of fit, a misrepresentation, misrecognition or mis-measurement that occurs 'in-between'. As the proverb tells us, 'there's many a slip twixt the cup and the lip'. However, the riddle of autoimmunity will not secure the status of an absence – the gap of the 'in-between' – by bookending either side of this break with some*thing*. It is the resuscitation of sovereign identity, as we have seen throughout this discussion, that I now want to explore by reading deconstruction *as* autoimmunity.

If we take deconstruction's identity as our departure point, or what makes it identifiable as a particular method among others, we find that quite a few practitioners enjoin us to consider 'the dusk of deconstruction', its fading away and purported replacement.[24] However, as Derrida notes in *Rogues* when explaining his use of the autoimmune, '[i]t consists not only in committing suicide but in compromising *sui-* or *self*-referentiality, the *self* or *sui-* of suicide itself'.[25] We could describe this as a thorough implosion of identity – which tends to install identity before its annihilation. Or we could read this implosion as originary, a force that generates identity in/as entanglement. With/in the 'illogical logic' of autoimmunity we can appreciate why Derrida might insist that deconstruction is not a method, or model of any*thing*; after all, the purported gap that secures and separates the analytical instrument from the subject who uses it and the object scrutinised is confounded in deconstruction. Derrida dilates on this theme in an interview with Richard Kearney.

> Deconstruction is not a philosophy or a method, it is not a phase, a period or a moment. It is something which is constantly at work and was at work before what we call 'deconstruction' started, so I cannot periodize. For me there is no 'after' deconstruction - not that I think that deconstruction is immortal - but for what I understand under the name deconstruction, there is no end, no beginning, and no after.[26]

More profoundly for this discussion, if there is no outside deconstruction, 'no outside text', then can the inner workings of this admitted *destinerrance* recuperate the sovereign, indeed, identity, in a way that might prove interesting for political analysis? I have mentioned the myriad ways in which critiques of sovereignty understand the problem as one of identity that loses integrity; that falls into error, failure and misrecognition. However, what difference does it make if our starting point is a sort of ecological involvement that has not lost its way because there is no proper way; an ecology that is so intricately enmeshed and all-encompassing that even those expressions (of itself) that appear circumscribed, isolated and autonomous, are 'themselves' generated by this generality? Referring back to Matzinger, this is not an ecology among others but 'One' whose systemic self-reference is capable of discrimination and individuation. If *différance* is the life pulse of this ecology, such that difference is and always was *différance*, then we are not dealing with an aggregation of entities that pre-exist their involvement. Indeed, we could say that this ecology's internal self-reference and self-recognition, its self-determination, undoes the clear division between health and threat, or even heteronomy and autonomy. But where does this leave us?

We might think that politics is no longer possible in this mired and messy landscape where foundations and commitments morph and meld into each other and b/orders dissolve before they are established. And yet, although I haven't arrived at a conclusion that will prove especially salutary for those who require definite answers, the intervention I am trying to make is far from nihilism. If we embark on a politics where what appears unique and specific is not immune from the general, not immured against ontological complicity because it is an expression of it, then this shift in the political landscape can prove effective against rigid assumptions about 'what goes without saying'. Of course, being forced to interrogate our terms of reference can be annoying because interminable, however the discovery that things can be different, that perhaps they are already different, can also prove sobering. An example of this was provided earlier in Ed Cohen's railing against those who confuse nature with culture. Cohen assumes that the only strategy to hand that can prevent a conservative biologism is to eschew the suggestion that biology could possibly *be* politically articulate. However, if nature is already culture then Cohen's fears are allayed, at least to some extent, even as it remains true that life, here biology, is argumentative, left *and* right-leaning, aggressive, ruthless, generous, self-sacrificing, caring...and in a constant state of transition and metamorphosis *because* its own self-reflections are volatile. It appears that the sovereign has returned *as* autoimmunity, and ironically, by implication, deconstruction assumes a sort of sovereign status in this ubiquitous animation – this 'no outside text' that is life.

It seems appropriate to close with Derrida on this very theme of life and the life sciences, where the 'subject' that practices this science is autoimmune – appearing as the 'object' of the study, and also as the representation or model, the third term that supposedly mediates the two separate entities.

> The message does not emit something, it says nothing, it communicates nothing; what it emits has the same structure as it, i.e. it is a message, and it is this emitted message that is going to allow the decipherment or translation of the emitting message, which implies the absence of anything outside the message, the information, the communication. This is why we have to be clear here that the words communication, information, message, are intra-textual and operate on condition of text, contrary to what they ordinarily lead one to think, namely that they communicate, emit or inform something.[27]

For Derrida, life structures itself through and as the arche-trace of differentiation. In order to be itself it is compelled to other itself and the difference is nothing at all!

Notes

[1] There are several versions of Katherine Craster's 'The Centipede's Dilemma', poem that speaks nicely to the paradoxical incoherence of subjectivity or personhood. We assume we are decision-making agents and yet we can't account for how those decisions are made. Of relevance here is Benjamin Libet's pioneering work in the 1980s on the neuroscience of volition. He observed an apparent lag between the neurological registration of decision-making activity – an unconscious 'decision' to flex a finger - and the conscious awareness of our intention to do so. On a first reckoning the experiments appear to confound what we mean by agency, and their interpretation is much debated as a consequence. Indeed, Libet himself was not persuaded that the results compromised individual freedom (See Libet, *Mind Time*).

[2] The notion of 'autoimmunity' fascinates researchers, even in the humanities and social sciences, because it destabilises the integrity of a departure point and the conventional logic of cause and effect. In simple terms, we tend to think of change as an external force – for example, time and the vicissitudes of life - that alters 'something' that was previously unchanged. However, the medical definition of autoimmunity presents us with a more complicated story: in this case, we learn that the integrity of the individual organism, or self, was never intact: 'The healthy human body is equipped with a powerful set of tools for resisting the onslaught of invading microorganisms (such as viruses, bacteria, and parasites). Unfortunately, this set of tools, known as the immune system, sometimes goes awry and attacks the body itself. These misdirected immune responses are referred to as autoimmunity, which can be demonstrated by the presence of autoantibodies or T lymphocytes reactive with host antigens.' (Johns Hopkins Autoimmune Disease Research Center). The implication here is not simply that this individual, or self, is also attacked from the inside. More alarmingly, a question arises about the very status of an individual if 'it' is constitutionally undone.

[3] For important historical references that introduce the problematic aspects of immunity discourse, see Haraway, "The Biopolitics of Postmodern Bodies," Martin, *Flexible Bodies* and Napier, *The Age of Immunology*.

[4] Osteoarthritis used to be explained in terms of external causes, such as 'wear and tear' on the joint, whereas rheumatoid arthritis was regarded as an autoimmune disease. Today, the former has also been described as an immune response. It is as if the body is reacting to a 'chronic wound' or protracted inflammation that it produces itself in the form of 'endogenous "danger signals"' (Scanzello, Plaas and Crow, "Innate immune system activation in osteoarthritis: is osteoarthritis a chronic wound?" 565). It has become routine in the medical literature to describe this perversity in terms of misrecognition. See also Orlowsky and Byers Kraus, "The Role of Innate Immunity in Osteoarthritis: When

Our First Line of Defense Goes on the Offensive."

[5] In Australia, a 'mere' handshake captured the nation's interest on the eve of the 2004 Federal Election. Mark Latham, the opposition hopeful, was seen to seize the then Prime Minister's hand, to yank him awkwardly with an inward jerk, and to then pump his arm with unseemly aggression. Even supporters saw the handshake as a sign of Latham's emotional immaturity and lack of statesmanship, and his aspirations were quickly dashed as a consequence. (See 'Mark Latham shakes John Howards hand').

[6] See Mackay, "Travels and Travails of Autoimmunity: A historical journey from discovery to rediscovery."

[7] Thomas Pradeu notes that Burnett remained uneasy about the distinction and offered alternatives towards the end of his life, however "unfortunately, these [Burnett's] revisions were paid scant attention by his contemporaries who remained, in their great majority, dedicated to the strict differentiation between self and non-self" (see *The Limits of the Self: Immunology and Biological Identity*, 81).

[8] Cited in Cohen, *A Body Worth Defending*, 26.

[9] Ibid., 27.

[10] Ibid.

[11] For a provocative and detailed analysis of *A Body Worth Defending*, see Jamieson, "The Politics of Immunity: Reading Cohen through Canguilhem and New Materialism."

[12] Matzinger in Cohen, *A Body Worth Defending*, 29.

[13] An interesting illustration of how such questions might pay dividends can be seen in the career move of astrophysicist, Paul Davies, into the medical sphere of cancer research. Quite specifically, his given task is to radically reconsider the ontological status of cancer. Although Davies doesn't discount the sense of cancer as threat, dysfunction and pathology, he qualifies this reading when he reminds us that cancer is inherent to all of life, even plants. For our purposes, it is interesting to note that the cellular behaviours of cancer are also described in terms of atavistic survival and endurance strategies, as if each cell can be seen as a lone entity whose most basic aspiration is to endure. Zeeya Merali, commenting on Davies' work, notes, '[Cancer] cells jettison higher functionality and switch their dormant ability to proliferate back on in a misguided attempt to survive. "Cancer is a fail-safe," Davies remarks. "Once the subroutine is triggered, it implements its program ruthlessly". (see Merali, "Physicists' model proposes evolutionary role for cancer"). What interests me here is that all cells carry these atavistic memories such that their 'true' program must comprehend an historical record whose triggers can sustain and sabotage at the same time. Given this, why do we assume that the life of each cell is, or *should* be, subordinated in some way to a larger biological entity whose sovereign existence demands it? Are terms such as 'atavistic', 'misguided', 'higher functionality' and 'program' justifiable if the identity of the sovereign self proves elusive?

[14] Cohen, *A Body Worth Defending*, 27.

[15] See Magnusson et al., "Relationships between diet-related changes in the gut microbiome and cognitive flexibility."

[16] Stauth, "High Fat and Sugar Diets May Lead to Loss of Cognitive Flexibility."

[17] See Wilson, *Gut Feminism*.

[18] Martone, "The Neuroscience of the Gut – *Strange but true: the brain is shaped by bacteria in the digestive tract*."

[19] Young, "Gut instincts: The secrets of your second brain."

[20] Smith, "Can the Bacteria in Your Gut Explain Your Mood?"

[21] Ibid.

[22] I note in passing that a recent issue of *New Scientist* (January 9, 2016) offers a rather dramatic example of why the *autos*, or sovereign self, cannot be immunised against the other. Under the compelling title, "Strangers within: meet the other humans who live in your body," we learn about the phenomenon of michrochimerism, which also has implications for immunity/autoimmunity. It seems that the barrier between mother and child in placentation is not absolute but strangely capricious, something which explains why cells with Y chromosomes can appear in the brains of mothers. I offer a brief description of just one aspect of such implications, aptly subtitled 'A family affair': 'Take, for example, a woman pregnant with a baby girl, her second child. We know that michrochimeric cells can stick around for decades, so it's easy to imagine cells from her eldest still running around her body. They could get transferred to

her new baby. If the eldest was a boy, the daughter now has cells from her brother. These could conceivably be passed on when the daughter has a child of her own – who would therefore have cells from their uncle' (Ridgway, "Strangers within: meet the other humans who live in your body"). I first came across this fascinating phenomenon in the work of Myra Hird ("Chimerism, mosaicism and the cultural construction of kinship") and Rebecca Yoshizawa (*Placentations: Agential Realism and the Science of Afterbirths*).

[23] Naas, "'One Nation…Indivisible: Jacques Derrida on the Autoimmunity of Democracy and the Sovereignty of God'," 18.

[24] Catherine Malabou's work is exemplary of this turn. See Malabou, *Plasticity at the Dusk of Writing: Dialectic, Destruction, Deconstruction*.

[25] Derrida, *Rogues: Two Essays on Reason*, 45.

[26] Derrida in Kearney, "Hospitality, Justice and Responsibility: A Dialogue with Jacques Derrida," 65.

[27] Derrida in Vitale, "The Text and the Living: Jacques Derrida between Biology and Deconstruction," 109.

Bibliography

Cohen, Ed. *A Body Worth Defending: Immunity, Biopolitics, and the Apotheosis of the Modern Body*. Durham: Duke University Press, 2009.

Craster, Katherine. "Pinafore Poems." *Cassell's Weekly* (1871).

Dawkins, Richard. *The Selfish Gene*. Oxford: Oxford University Press, 1976.

Derrida, Jacques. *Rogues: Two Essays on Reason*. Translated by Pascale-Anne Brault and Michael Naas. Stanford: Stanford University Press, 2005.

Haraway, Donna. "The Biopolitics of Postmodern Bodies: Determinations of Self in Immune System Discourse." *Differences: A Journal of Feminist Cultural Studies* 1, no. 1 (1989): 3–43.

Hird Myra. "Chimerism, mosaicism and the cultural construction of kinship." *Sexualities* 7 (2004): 217–232.

Jamieson, Michelle. "The Politics of Immunity: Reading Cohen through Canguilhem and New Materialism." *Body & Society* (2015).

Johns Hopkins Autoimmune Disease Research Center. Accessed July 12, 2016. http://autoimmune.pathology.jhmi.edu/whatisautoimmunity.html

Kearney, Richard. "Hospitality, Justice and Responsibility: A Dialogue with Jacques Derrida." In *Questioning Ethics: Contemporary Debates in Philosophy*, edited by Richard Kearney and Mark Dooley, 65–83. New York, NY: Routledge, 1998.

Libet, Benjamin. *Mind Time: The Temporal Factor in Consciousness*. Cambridge Mass: Harvard University Press, 2004.

Mackay, Ian R. "Travels and Travails of Autoimmunity: A historical journey from discovery to rediscovery." *Autoimmunity Reviews* 9 (2010): A251-A258.

Magnusson, K. R., et al. "Relationships between diet-related changes in the gut microbiome and cognitive flexibility." *Neuroscience* 300 (2015).

Malabou, Catherine. *Plasticity at the Dusk of Writing: Dialectic, Destruction, Deconstruction*. New York, NY: Columbia University Press, 2010.

'Mark Latham shakes John Howards hand'. Accessed July 12, 2016. https://www.youtube.com/watch?v=Wh7HoB1SmKU

Martin, Emily. *Flexible Bodies: Tracking Immunity in American Culture - From the Days of Polio to the Age of AIDS*. Boston, MA: Beacon Press, 1994.

Martone, Robert. "The Neuroscience of the Gut – *Strange but true: the brain is shaped by bacteria in the digestive tract*." *Scientific American* 23 (2011). Accessed September 5, 2016. http://www.scientificamerican.com/article/the-neuroscience-of-gut/

Merali, Zeeya. 2014. "Physicists' model proposes evolutionary role for cancer." *Nature*, October 2. http://www.nature.com/news/physicists-model-proposes-evolutionary-role-for-cancer-1.16068

Naas, Michael. ""One Nation…Indivisible: Jacques Derrida on the Autoimmunity of Democracy and the Sovereignty of God'." *Research in Phenomenology* 36 (2006): 15–44.

Napier, A. David. *The Age of Immunology: Conceiving a Future in an Alienating World*. Chicago and London: The University of Chicago Press, 2003.

Orlowsky, Eric W. and Byers Kraus, V. "The Role of Innate Immunity in Osteoarthritis: When Our First Line of Defense Goes on the Offensive." *Journal of Rheumatology* 42, no. 3 (2015): 363-71.

Pradeu, Thomas. *The Limits of the Self: Immunology and Biological Identity*. Translated by Elizabeth Vitanza. Oxford and New York: Oxford University Press, 2012.

Ridgway, Andy. "Strangers within: meet the other humans who live in your body." *New Scientist* (January 9, 2016). Accessed September 5, 2016. https://www.newscientist.com/article/mg22930550-400-strangers-within-meet-the-other-humans-who-live-in-your-body/

Scanzello, Carla R., Plaas, Anna and Crow, Mary K. "Innate immune system activation in osteoarthritis: is osteoarthritis a chronic wound?" *Current Opinion in Rheumatology* (2008).

Smith, Peter Andrey. "Can the Bacteria in Your Gut Explain Your Mood?" *The New York Times* (June 23, 2015). Accessed September 5, 2016. http://www.nytimes.com/2015/06/28/magazine/can-the-bacteria-in-your-gut-explain-your-mood.html?_r=0

Stauth, David. "High Fat and Sugar Diets May Lead to Loss of Cognitive Flexibility." *Neuroscience News* (June 22, 2915). Accessed September 5, 2016. http://neurosciencenews.com/diet-gut-bacteria-cognition-2147/

Vitale, Francesco. "The Text and the Living: Jacques Derrida between Biology and Deconstruction." *The Oxford Literary Review* 36, no. 1 (2014): 95–114.

Wilson, Elizabeth. *Gut Feminism*. Durham NC: Duke University Press, 2015.

Yoshizawa, Rebecca Scott. *Placentations: Agential Realism and the Science of Afterbirths*. PhD Dissertation. Queen's University Kingston, Ontario, 2014.

Young, Emma. "Gut instincts: The secrets of your second brain." *New Scientist* (December 12, 2012). Accessed September 5, 2016. https://www.newscientist.com/article/mg21628951-900-gut-instincts-the-secrets-of-your-second-brain/

Cosmic Topologies of Imitation: From the Horror of Digital Autotoxicus to the Auto-Toxicity of the Social

Tony D. Sampson

This article expands on an earlier concept of horror autotoxicus linked to digital contagions of spam and network *Virality*.[1] It aims to present, as such, a broader conception of cosmic topologies of imitation (CTI) intended to better grasp the relatively new practices of social media marketing. Similar to digital autotoxicity, CTI provide the perfect medium for sharing while also spreading contagions that can potentially contaminate the medium itself. However, whereas digital contagions are perhaps limited to the toxicity of a technical layer of information viruses, the contagions of CTI are an all-pervasive auto-toxicity which can infect human bodies and technologies increasingly in concert with each other. This is an exceptional autotoxicus that significantly blurs the immunological line of exemption between self and nonself, and potentially, the anthropomorphic distinction between individual self and collective others.

This earlier work on digital culture discussed the significant role of contagion in virus writing cultures and online communication practices, where, in short, the tendency for codes and communication messages to spread like viruses on a network inspired an extremely profitable anti-virus industry and nascent viral marketing business. On the one hand, biological analogies ushered in an anti-virus discursive formation that determined, to some extent, what people can and cannot do on a network by distinguishing between good and bad digital code in a similar way to which organic immune systems are assumed to exempt the threat posed by anomalous nonself cells from those of the self. On the other hand though, prediscursive forces were identified in the social spreading of biologically derived anxieties, linked to these appeals to immunity, and efforts made to trigger affective contagions associated with viral marketing practices. Indeed, in many ways the concept of horror autotoxicus was initially introduced as a way to explain how immunologic-inspired digital systems become vulnerable to viral communication environments in which contagious anomalies are constituent rather than exempt. In this context, autoimmunity is a useful concept because it challenges the immunologic principles of the self/nonself binary relation and helps to identify discursive formations and prediscursive forces that arrange social relations by way of contamination rather than immunity. Indeed, taken forward to an all-pervasive corporate social media era in which a second wave of viral marketing has arguably come of age, this article revisits horror autotoxicus to argue that the virality of digital culture can now be grasped through a prevailing auto-toxicity of the social.

In a very concrete fashion the now infamous Facebook research on emotional contagion in 2014 (discussed below) evidences how a continued focus on contagion theory adds to a much needed critical study of digital culture. The rise of corporate social media in the last decade has indeed necessitated a reenergizing of these critical approaches. Langlois and Elmer distinguish between three different yet intertwined approaches that are significant to this discussion.[2] Firstly, the virality of social media is closely related to a critical economy approach that understands corporate endeavours to mine social life through appeals to such things as emotional, felt and affective user experiences with software. Social media does more than merely capture the attention of users and sell it on to marketers. It produces user performances that marketers can readily mine, manipulate and nudge into action. Secondly, the conceptual work developed in this article is directly linked to empirical work focused on the algorithms that function behind the scenes on social media platforms. The conceptualization of CTI therefore recognizes how capricious affective contagions are nudged into action by way of analytics triggered by, for example, a click on a like or share button. Lastly, by helping to illuminate the manipulation of affective user experiences at the interface of corporate social media this discussion feeds into a third software activist approach to corporate social media with a view to awakening 'new user agencies'[3] beyond those social relations already configured by corporate marketers.

Rethinking Immunity through Autoimmunity

Autoimmunity is a concept that explores beyond earlier territorializations of immunological exemption to ever more complex stratagems that tap into contagious social arrangements in digital culture. Yet, it is important to begin by noting that autoimmunity is not opposed to immunologic. To grasp its full purchase we need to approach autoimmunity by thinking through immunology. As set out in this special issue, autoimmunity is conventionally studied within the field of immunology. The concept refers to an immunologic phenomenon whereby an organism mounts an immune response against its own tissues; a paradoxical situation in which self-defence (immunity, protection) manifests as self-harm (pathology). Today, the term autoimmunity is used to account for any instance in which the body fails to recognise its own constituents as 'self', an error that results in self-harm or injury.

Autoimmunity is, however, regarded as a controversial concept within immunology. It is important, as such, to grasp the flaws in Paul Ehrlich's original concept of horror autotoxicus. To begin with, in crude terms autoimmunity is posited as an impossibility because all organisms are so horrified by self-discrimination that they will selectively avoid self-toxicity. The later discovery of the harsh realities of autoimmune disease demonstrates deep problems in the natural preservation of an organic unity based on the overriding rule of self-tolerance. There are nonetheless those working in immunology who argue that Ehlrich's theory is misunderstood and that while self-tolerance is evidently the rule, autoimmunity is always the exception.[4] Moreover, it is further argued that rather than being a destructive incongruity of the immune system, the exception is always implicated in the maintenance of the rule.[5] In other words, the self-destructive anomaly is considered to play a productive role in the evolutionary survival of the organism.

Putting evolutionary determined equilibrium aside for now, the paradoxical relation between self and nonself in autoimmunity problematizes the assumed emergence of a natural state of immunity. The defences provided by the horror of self-toxicity will, on occasion, acquiesce, and the exception will overrule self-tolerance, possibly leading to the exceptional destruction of the organism. There is an ongoing debate concerning the value of the self/non-self metaphor as a theoretical tool to understand how cellular organisms defend against infections in immunology. For some, the metaphor's value plunged when it became evident that cells have the potential to be simultaneously anti-self and anti-foreign. Indeed, cellular behaviour seems to defy the terms set out by the immunological metaphor. As Robert S. Schwartz puts it, 'the immune system, in short, does not operate by anthropomorphic principles such as "learn," "self," and "foreign," nor is there a sharp line between "self" and "foreign"'.[6]

Taking this challenge to immunologic a step further, autoimmunity also questions how these same anthropomorphic principles are assumed to arrange social relations. In other words, similarly considered in terms of a broader concept, autoimmunity significantly complicates notions of communication, defence and regulation conventionally understood as immunologic processes. Hence, the concept prompts a novel approach that questions the ordering of social relations according to self/other relations. It tests the permeability of borders assumed to exist between self-identity and threats posed by an anomalous destructive nonself. As such, autoimmunity introduces a politics of exception, which unlike the negative binarisms of immunological exemption, can be grasped as an affirmative process.

The destructive and productive role of the viral anomaly in digital culture has been described as a topological spatiotemporal autotoxicity.[7] This is 'a condition akin to a *horror autotoxicus* of the digital network', wherein the 'capacity of the network to propagate its own imperfections exceeds the metaphor with natural unity'.[8] Considered in stark contrast to immunologic, the topology of the digital network is the 'perfect medium' for spreading both 'perfection and imperfection'.[9] The goal now, it would seem (given that the virality of the digital network has become ever more interwoven with the social in so many profound ways), is to question how a more generalized concept of autoimmunity might be applied to social arrangements that occur when bodies and technologies are increasingly in concert with each other. Beyond digital contagion, it would seem, we encounter CTI. This is not just a digital infrastructure that confuses self and nonself, but mixtures of technologies and bodies that become socially arranged according to autotoxicity.

The notion that self/nonself relations are in a perpetual state of paradox is evidently nothing new. In order to grasp autoimmunity in this broader topological sense we do not need to look much further than Gabriel Tarde to resuscitate a social theory in which capricious contagious overspills are not regarded as anomalous, but become key to the arrangement of everyday social relations.[10] Along these lines, relations do not simply become contagious; they are contagions. The arrangement of everyday relations established between humans and the world they inhabit are determined, as follows, by Tarde's imitative radiation. The CTI concept expands on this notion to ask what happens to the concept of self-identity when, as Tarde argued, the psychological sense of 'myself' is considered to be contaminated by the imitations of others.[11] In other words, what happens when the self is understood to imitate the other to a point at which the relation between self and other – so important to both immunologic and anthropomorphic principles – collapses into a social cosmos of imitative relationality? Moreover, what occurs to social arrangements when the exception of self-toxicity is no longer considered an anomaly, but becomes the rule? Indeed, in a twenty first century social media world dominated by the contaminating sensory environments of market capitalism, it is arguably no longer self-harm that should concern us, but a tendency toward what Roger Caillois calls collective masochism.[12] To establish this theoretical perspective I will again look to manifestations of digital culture; specifically, in this case, social media marketing, as a way to grasp how CTI can be used to rethink an age that is increasingly defined by radical self/nonself relations encountered in contagious social arrangements.

Mirrors, Mimicry and Marketing

Before exploring what the concept of CTI can achieve, it is necessary to trace the ways in which self/other relations have featured in academic marketing literature. To be begin with, it is important to note that a Tardean approach has made some impact on the study of marketing in terms of grasping, for example, the significance of pass-on-power, as well as co-production, affect and sentiment in consumption.[13] But for the most part there is a marked tendency in more industry focused literature in particular to analyze the self-concept in conventional ways that render it discrete in terms of how it interacts with others in sensory environments. At first glance, this discreteness is subtly conceived of. For instance, according to a recent academic study of adolescent photo sharing on social media the self and its interaction with others in the external world is considered 'integral to the creation and continuation of a stable harmonious self-concept'.[14] Adolescents in particular are assumed to upload and share photos of themselves adorned in various products as a way to crystalize the formation of their self-identity to present to others.[15] However, this account of identity formation relies on a supposition that although self-identity admits to social relations, the inner sense of self exists regardless of the external world.[16] The notion that adolescents mimic others they encounter, by way of adorning similar cloths, is often downplayed, as such. In this kind of account the other functions mainly as a kind of collective mirror to help the adolescent grapple with the question: who am I? Group associations are important, but the self-concept is defined predominantly by representational internal choices made about these social associations, alongside apparently wilful consumption preferences for clothing, jargon and music taste, for example.

This supposition is challenged by Tarde who insists that the imitations we find in these external relations should be the main focus of social theory. Indeed, Tarde countered individual and collective representations by presupposing 'exactly what needs explaining, namely, "the similarity of millions of people."'[17] This is why, Deleuze and Guattari contend, 'Tarde was interested instead in the world of detail, or of the infinitesimal: the little imitations, oppositions and inventions constituting an entire realm of subrepresentative matter'.[18] From a Tardean perspective there is indeed no need for a representational mirror to ensure that collective mimicry takes place. Arguably these mirroring processes present nothing more than a dream-of-action that supports an illusory boundary line between inner psychological experience of self and the outer world. To be sure, the aim of current social media marketing strategies is not, arguably, to infect the desire for a stable sense of the self, but rather leech the porosity of the psychological self-image to the imitative radiations of the external world. It is this porosity to imitation that is readily exploited by marketers able to tap into big data assemblages providing a trace of (and adding a value to) what is imitated i.e. trending, shared, liked, etc. That is to say, social media marketers do not infect the self, but rather harvest and activate a contagious social medium. It is this Tardean tendency toward social contamination and imitative radiation that marketers readily tap into (and encourage) in order to develop strategies of social influence.

Before expanding more on this tendency it is necessary to further grasp the role mirrors and mimicry have played in critical approaches to marketing that in many ways echo the immunologic. The inclination to lean on discrete concepts of self/other relations in recent marketing literature can certainly be traced back to much earlier attempts to decode the ideology of marketers working mainly in advertising in the 1960s and 70s. For instance, Judith Williamson's radical thesis on advertising introduces the Lacanian influenced concept of the 'Created Self'; arguing that the ideological intention of the marketer is to bring together groups of consumers, while at the same time individuating (and alienating) them.[19] That is, creating a brand message that becomes an integrated part of a coherent sense of self to a point wherein the self becomes a commodity. Adverts that feature *Pepsi People*, for example, create an imaginary social medium, which offers the individual a Lacanian mirror-image of the external world to gaze into and aspire to.[20] It is the aim of marketers to draw consumers into a desire to become one of the *Pepsi People* in order to feel good. But, evidently, such social aspirations and desires for perpetual happiness are delusional. This is how ideology is supposed to simultaneously provide a false image to mimic, while also individuating and alienating the sense of self. Indeed, Williamson sees Lacan's mirror as a metaphor for the external reflection of the self that advertisers produce – an ersatz imitation of sorts – encountered in the external world that estranges the self from the other.[21] Nonetheless, despite its recognition of the external world, ideological advertising is significantly grasped like a mechanism of infection in which 'it is so crucial for the ad to enter you, and exist inside rather than outside your self-image: in fact, to create it'.[22] Like the basis of Lacan's account of the mirror-image, the organism is, at first, so captivated by the external environment that it becomes its camouflage. In other words, mimicry is the capture of the organism by the environment rather than some evolutionary necessity to mimic surroundings in order to survive. But eventually this loss of self to the external world through captivation is transferred from the externality of the environment – bodily affects, camouflage, etc. – to the inner world of phantasy, the narcissism of the ego and its false identification with the other. This is how, in short, bodily affects become phantasy in Lacan's mirror stage.

To expand on this point we can see how differences and resemblances become important factors in determining an individuated self/other relation in the ideological analysis of advertising. Resemblances are located in the mirror images of people that appeal to you: people like you. Adolescent and adult consumers can, as such, compare themselves to the other, creating a sense of coherence that resonates with the brands they consume. But, at the same time, differences in ideological analysis are also found in the semiotic signification of the self/other relation. That is to say, the glimpse of the other (in the mirror-image of the ad) points to what you cannot be. Just as one cannot occupy the space of the mirror, one can never be happy all of the time. So despite the mimicry, the mirror-image makes consumers aware of what they are not. It makes them cognizant of their separation from the other and the environment they inhabit.[23] Advertising is not only an infection of the inner world, it applies a kind of immunologic exemption to self/other relations insofar as the mirror-image isolates self from nonself and self from external world; producing an illusory, but stable sense of a narcissistic self-identity into which products and brands can be readily inserted. To be sure, Williamson regards the dream of a coherent self to be the object of the consumer's desire. Marketing consequently feeds on this desire for what is ultimately an unobtainable stability. This is the ideological creation of an infected self-concept, wherein the sense of self becomes a product in itself; the creation of a commodified self, no less.

There are some important variations in the ideological-semiotic analysis of advertising and Tarde's imitation thesis that need to be ironed out before we can fully explore autoimmunity. To begin with, although similar in some respects to Williamson's account, insofar as the object of desire is an illusory sense of self, what composes the dream of action in Tarde's society of imitation is not determined by a Lacanian mirror that gives rise to the representation of I. On the contrary, the object of Tardean desire is always belief. Again, there are subtle differences here that need to be considered. While beliefs may seem to offer a sense of inner stability, what is believed in is always imitated from the beliefs of others. The illusory sense of self acquired through mimicry is not therefore a representation of I in a mirror, but a contagious flow of imitated belief experienced at a sub-representational level. In other words, the sense of an inner coherence or self-identity, which seems to separate the inner world from the external world, is the illusion. It is a dream of volition; a sense of self experienced in the reverie of social associations. The beliefs that are mimicked, that are imagined to belong to a self, belong to a social medium.

To further think through these differences in immunologically orientated terms, it is important to go back to the origins of Williamson's use of the Lacanian mirror. Lacan was famously inspired by Caillois's work on insects, fish, octopi and mantises, and his significant challenge to the prevalent idea that mimicry is an instinctual form of protective immunity brought about by threats posed to the organism from the outside world. That is to say, the adaptable surface (or skin) of the animal becomes the first level of immunological defence. Rather than seeing these surface mimicries as protection for the organism against the external threat of the other, Caillois alternatively points to the many vulnerabilities that arise when the surface of an organism takes on the visual properties of its environment. The remains of mimetic insects are indeed as abundant in the stomachs of predators as those that cannot change their visual appearance.[24] Caillois therefore begins to rethink the organism's mimicry of the environment not as a survival tactic, but as a capture of the subject in the spatial coordinates of its surroundings; an individual captured in a topology. As Jussi Parikka notes, 'Caillois addressed the function of mimicry not as a representation of figures or space but a spatial assemblage that bordered on disorder'.[25] Mimicry is all about 'bodies in interaction' with the environment; that is, a relation between the haptic visual properties of space and affected bodies.[26] Indeed, Parikka goes on to ponder a notion of affective relationality that in many ways counters the mirror stage insofar as it draws attention to the porous nature of the inside/outside relation to such an extent that the representational I is replaced by the space of the environment.[27] The inner and outer world of phenomenological experience is therefore collapsed into an external world of affective relationality that disturbs the relation between personality and space. 'The reflective mind is forced to follow the noncognitive knowledge and motility of the body [...] [Caillois thus provides] a nonphenomenological mode of understanding the lived topology of the event'.[28]

Williamson's approach borrows from Lacan's reading of Caillois to argue that the outside image alienates the psychological self. However, a distinction needs to be made between the notion of advertising entering into, and occupying, the inner world of the consumer and a counter notion of a mimicry of bodily affects that challenges the self-concept by locating social relations in a sensory environment. In other words, the ideological critique insists on the production of an inner personality (however delusional) while a nonphenomenological approach offers a theory of subjectivity produced by the capturing of individuals in space. The changes on the surface of the organism's body need not therefore become internalized in a reflective mind. As Caillois puts it, 'the feeling of personality, considered as the organism's feeling of distinction from its surroundings, of the connection between consciousness and a particular point in space, cannot fail under these conditions to be seriously undermined'.[29]

There also needs to be a historical footnote added to this discussion which entertains a considerably older notion of infectious social relations and its increasing relevance to an understanding of social media marketing today. Indeed, again, there is nothing entirely new here. Although the apparent contagiousness of the nineteenth century crowds that inform Tarde's imitation thesis predate the mediated publics of the twentieth century, the objectives of twenty first century social media marketers seem to exhibit the same externalized contagious tendencies he recognized. From this perspective, marketers do not need to infiltrate the self via the mirrors and mimicry of ideology, but instead they tap into the contagious social medium in which consumer beliefs about products and brands are readily passed on as affective contagions. As follows, marketing is not the creation of self-identity, but rather the production of sensory environments in which the contagions of a social medium can be encouraged. The social medium becomes the product. Social media is indeed an invention which appropriates desires always-already spreading through the external world.

Social Media Marketing as Autoimmunity

The potential exploitation of a contagious social medium can be readily observed in an experiment carried out by Facebook in 2014. This involved the manipulation of the emotional content of news feeds and measuring the effect these manipulations had on the emotions of 689,003 members of the social media phenomenon in terms of how contagious they became.[30] The researchers who carried out the experiment found that when they reduced the positive expressions displayed by other users they produced less positive and more negative posts. Likewise, when negative expressions were reduced, the opposite pattern occurred. Although the recorded levels of contagion were rather paltry the researchers concluded that the 'emotions expressed by others on Facebook influence our own emotions, constituting experimental evidence for massive-scale contagion via social networks'.[31] Indeed, even if this contentious and unethical attempt by Facebook to influence moods produced meagre evidence of contagion, the design and implementation of the experiment itself should alert us to a potentially Huxleyesque mode of mass manipulation. As Nicolas Carr contends, the bizarrely titled

'Experimental Evidence of Massive-Scale Emotional Contagion' through Social Networks draws attention to the way in which the cultivation of big data by marketers treats human subjects like lab rats while also pointing to the widespread nature of manipulation by social media companies. 'What was most worrisome about the study', Carr contends, 'lay not in its design or its findings, but in its ordinariness'.[32] This kind of research is indeed part of a 'visible tip of an enormous and otherwise well-concealed iceberg' in the social media industry.[33] To be sure, the one thing that both the disparagers and apologists for social media seem to agree on is that user manipulation is rife on the internet. It is, after all, what every social media business enterprise strives to do.

Social media networks are the perfect medium for sharing and, it would seem, a test bed, or nursery, for cultivating and igniting emotional contagions. Unlike broadcast media, which similarly spread emotions, the users of these networks are predisposed, it would seem, to routinely share their feelings in exchange for the tools that allow them to freely do so without concern for how these tools might, in turn, be used to manipulate them. Of course, despite the relatively small scale media storm of outrage surrounding this particular attempt to manipulate emotions, many Facebook users will be oblivious to their participation in this research, or indeed, their assumed inclination to respond to emotional suggestion in such an apparently porous and imitative fashion. Moreover, most Facebook users will be unaware of the role their ignited emotional responses play in an infectious social medium; oblivious to the way in which emotions are being harvested in the data assemblages mined by corporate social media.

Beyond these ethical concerns, Facebook's emotional contagion research can also be grasped as part of a trajectory of digital autoimmunity. Indeed, ever since the invention of the online marketplace, marketers have arguably striven to emulate the infectiousness of biological and computer viruses so as to surreptitiously spread marketing messages through social networks unawares. These efforts can be seen as part of two waves of viral marketing in which marketers have increasingly relied on the idea that an infected host will pass on a message more effectively through its own networks than it would through conventional media channels. Although the ignition of virality is never certain, in the first wave, the low cost of viral marketing was a good enough incentive, it would seem, for business enterprises to switch from expensive broadcast media to viral networks. Moreover, the prospect of evading the conscious tyranny of mass marketing by simultaneously secreting away messages in everyday communications and turning consumers into the medium for potential contagions also offered novel unconscious neural pathways for marketers to spread their messages.

The Facebook research on emotional contagion represents a considerable development on the immunological and memetic theoretical models that underpinned the first wave of cost effective viral marketing. Indeed, whereas the template for the first wave was based on a configuration of virulent memes and immunological disease thresholds the second wave seems to sidestep the defensive horror of autotoxicus by looking to collapse the immunological distinctions between self, nonself and the social medium in which they become assembled. Perhaps this shift from a first to a second wave of viral marketing can be best observed in recent challenges to the immunologic model posed from within marketing itself.[34] This is a challenge to the notion that the trigger for contagious overspills can be found in network clusters that develop around influential and promiscuous individuals. Here Malcolm Gladwell's crude version of threshold theory is used to explain the point at which a small trend tips over into a big contagion. That is, wherein the number of infected nodes outlives the number of uninfected nodes. A mainstay of viral marketing, Gladwell's *Tipping Point* thesis is nevertheless confronted by Duncan Watts's contention that contagions are the product of the 'infectability of the networked world'.[35] This is a point of departure that has not been overlooked by social media marketers. The research focus has in fact significantly shifted away from influential nodes toward the design and production of infectable small world networks that prime mood and ignite capricious affective contagions.[36]

Despite initial claims to have captured what gets passed on in a social network in practical terms, first wave viral marketing was still pushing messages out to an online audience paying attention to websites in much the same way as they would mass media. Designers were engaged in producing sticky experiences that encouraged the cultural practice of passing on content. The big difference with social media today is that it encourages the passing on of viral content through such tactics as following, liking, sharing etc., ensuring that complex and capricious contagions are more readily mined and prompted into action. In current big data research there is a continuing focus on producing small changes intended to lead to large scale contagions. For example, in the work of Watts we see how exceptional contagions are, and how, as such, the affective priming and manipulation of the mood of the social medium becomes the main focus. It is therefore not the infected subject that matters, but rather the capricious encounters in affective atmospheres that might ignite contagion.

Autoimmunity as Collective Masochism

To add a Tardean slant to these developments, we might say that the second wave of viral marketing denotes the dissolution of the infected subject into CTI. The infectious mimicry of autoimmunity is, as such, no longer (borrowing from immunology again) about self-harm; it is perhaps, following Caillois, all about collective masochism: a phenomenon he located in the sensory environments of mimicking animals.

> [T]here are cases in which mimicry causes the creature to go from bad to worse: geometer-moth caterpillars simulate shoots of shrubbery so well that gardeners cut them with their

> pruning shears. The case of the Phyllia is even sadder: they browse among themselves, taking each other for real leaves, in such a way that one might accept the idea of a sort of collective masochism leading to mutual homophagy, the simulation of the leaf being a provocation to cannibalism in this kind of totem feast.[37]

The point is that as the market colonizes and absorbs the sensory environment in which human mimicry takes place, these molecular imitations will inevitably become more oriented toward mimicking products and brands. In other words, mimicry is an outcome of the capture of subjectivity by the space of the market. Significantly, this is not a subject that can freely identify with an I within space, since it is the space itself that positions the subject in the market. Unlike Williamson's focus on commodification of the self, which occurs inside the subject, we need to look to the topological relations that capture subjectivity. This point can be expanded upon by returning to the adolescent photo-sharing experiences discussed above. We can see here how young consumers, adorned in the products and brands they find in the shopping malls, spread their mimicry of the sensory environment via social media to CTI that prompt more consumers to become coordinates in the topological grid of the market. In classic Tardean terms then, this is imitative radiation; it is a molecular mimicry that helps to explain the similarity of millions of people. As Caillois similarly puts it, we find a kind of magic attraction in these topologies in which 'like produces like'.[38]

In the first wave of viral marketing the infected body becomes the marketing message. It is, in itself, the virus that passes on the message. The infected body becomes the host medium of contagion. In the second wave the relation between self and nonself has not only become more blurred in a topological sense; it has also been captured by the space of the market. It is not the body, but the social medium that is now the virus. Indeed, by way of occupying the sensory environments in which relations are made, the market has laid down the spatial and temporal conditions of social arrangements. It influences, in this way, what gets imitated and what gets passed on. Williamson's response to this capture of subjectivity by the space of the market is to try to decode the infected self; that is to say, grasp the creation of the self by the market. The intention is, it seems, to provide the individual with the semiotic tools with which to see through the ideological trickery of advertising. However, when consumers become the medium of infection the sense of an inside being infiltrated by an outside becomes lost in the spatial capture of a topology. There is no incoming message to decode. Indeed, consumers are no longer able to decode marketing messages since they have become participants in an infectable space in which they co-produce and pass on code. The second wave is profound in this sense, since it is no longer the market that directly infects, but consumer collectives that indirectly infect others. Facebook's emotional research creates, as such, a topology, not a self, in which looping affective relations, ignited by online content (newsfeeds), spread through pass-on power. The big data lab rat unconsciously becomes part of a mischief of rats oblivious to the viruses they carry and seemingly insensible to the prospect of becoming an active carrier for brand messages.

Autoimmunity, Anxiety and Transindividuality

Becoming viral is still a practice embraced in marketing circles, which builds on the popular discourses of gurus like Gladwell and Watts and is sold on as a commodity in the form of the best seller, the business seminar and Ted Talk. But a second wave of viral marketing needs to be grasped as part of a more general and shifting immunological discursive formation, which at first territorialized populations around the visceral fear of the nonself, but now ignites a wider range of contagions including many joyful encounters with affective capitalism. Yet, despite this reorientation, immunologic anxiety has not entirely disappeared from view. The blissfully unaware Facebook lab rats might one day wake up from their somnambulistic stupor. The anxiety experienced will not be the outcome of a realization that the sense of self has been occupied by the market because, as we have seen, this is not the nature of the spatial capture of subjectivity. The anxiety felt will, in contrast, be experienced through the terrifying apprehension that the space occupied (and mimicked) is a dream of action. Indeed, as is argued below, it is the conditions of CTI in the social medium itself that causes new anxieties to unfold. Social media activists and researchers alike need to therefore better understand the dynamics of this topological spatial capture.

The relational arrangements between individuals and the topological space they occupy requires a radical rethink. Developing on Parikka's reading of Gilbert Simondon, we might begin by considering CTI not as a spatial backdrop in which communication takes place, but rather as 'an active milieu of relations'.[39] This is a topological space that mediatizes the individual; producing intensive individuation processes that 'situate the subject in the world'.[40] In the novel social arrangements of this space, the prediscursive anxieties relating to contagion experienced in the immunologic model are substituted by new anxieties concerning the extent to which already infected bodies become part of a seemingly inescapable contagious social medium. That is, a sudden realization that what was regarded as a sense of ownership over the psychological self, which seemed to belong to the I, is in fact part of a shared data assemblage steered by the market researchers at Facebook. The trending posts we saw that made us laugh, get angry and cry; the posts we passed on to our friends and followers as shares and likes. They were mostly ersatz experiences. This is a moment of anxiety when the individual becomes aware that they are part of a collective virus and actively engaged in passing it on by way of their interactions with others. These are moments of anxiety when individuals become 'aware of their presence as part of the "informational collective" that shapes online activity' and emotional experiences.[41] This is perhaps akin to a Simondonian anxiety wherein the difference between individuality and collectivity collapses into an affective state of transindividuality.[42]

Immunity to Relational Media

Back in 2006, the information architect and design consultant, Adam Greenfield, drew our attention to a near future digital culture in which ubiquitous computing makes everyday life 'fiercely relational'.[43] Pervasive computing introduces a lived relationality that is not simply experienced when individuals become a set of values stored in a database. This is already a reality we find in our experiences with social media. But it will also increasingly be realized in the way in which such values, including spatial proximity to points of consumption, location traces and emotional dispositions, are matched against the values belonging to others. As computing becomes ever more ubiquitous these relational values will exert a 'transformative influence' on social relations.[44] Indeed, if we are to follow, as Greenfield does, Erving Goffman's notion that we are all actors wearing a collection of masks we switch between in order to manage self-identities exposed to ever changing social situations, then we need to grasp how relational media threatens to make the sustaining of different masks 'untenable'.[45] In the age of social media, the personal in computing has certainly moved into the social domain where the private and public performances of Goffman's masked actors collapse into data-bodies assembled by relational databases.

Beyond Greenfield's account, however, we might also venture that relational media draws attention to a much older problem than who controls the 'custody of self-consciousness'.[46] That is, the problem of what happens to individual and collective experiences when exposed to all-pervasive technology. This problem clearly maps onto the shift in immunological orientation highlighted in this article. Indeed, given the proclivity of social media, and pervasive computing, toward autotoxicity, it is the relational aspects of immunology, particularly with regard to the sensory relations established between humans and technology, which require attention. It is therefore Ellis and Tucker's recent social psychology reading of Simondon's technics that I now conclude with, since as they appropriately claim, not enough work had been done on this relation.[47] To begin with, the point needs to be made that although social media adapts the way in which a person experiences individuating events, following Simondon, the focus on the individual must not be confused with the constituted being. Thus as personal life increasingly shifts from individuals to the huge databases of governments and commercial organizations, the intersection between humans and technology unfolds as part of processes of individuation, which do not have to be human.[48] As Ellis and Tucker note, Simondon does not ontologically, as such, separate bodies and technology because both are part of the experience of individuation.[49] Indeed, human and technological individuations are the threshold point at which human dreams and machines become mixed. However, this is not to say that a nightmarish tension or deep anxiety does not exist in this coming together of bodily and technological arrangements. As they assemble, something novel and unknown emerges.

As is the case with immunology, the psychic self becomes a conceptual problem that cannot be defined by internal properties alone. It is rather an affective relation, produced through processes, not separate categories. Similarly, like Tarde's imitative subjectivity, an individual 'always-already carries some of the collective with it'.[50] The resulting anxiety is not therefore equivalent to the alienation established between immunological self and nonself, nor is it, for that matter, akin to Williamson's alienating mirror image. On the contrary, this is anxiety felt as an outcome of the 'coming together' of technologies and bodies, forming new collective arrangements and experiences that challenge immunological, and potentially anthropomorphic, divisions. This is not a tension-free experience, since the individual psyche always-already experiences collective baggage as an anxiety. In autoimmunity terms this is perhaps a new kind of horror that emerges through an experience that is both individual and collective – self and nonself – at the same time. That is what Simondon refers to as the preindividual. In other words, anxiety arises through an unresolvable perceptual problem of individuation and preindividuation. This occurs because of 'the reality that the individual experiences itself as a unique subject, but at the same time recognises itself as partially collective'.[51] Returning to the example of the Facebook lab rat, it is the revelatory experience of realizing that our emotional experiences are not ours that produces a new horror.

How then to overcome the anxieties ignited in the experiences of CTI? One consideration might be to continue to follow Simondon's solution to anxiety in the concept of the transindividual. This is not a reconstitution of individual or collective categories. As Ellis and Tucker point out, anxiety cannot be resolved inside the subject or the collective.[52] It requires a perceptual bridge that might enable a softer passage through the individual-collective continuum. This is a bridge that counters internal and external spaces, working across boundaries of self and nonself. Moreover, the transindividual escapes spatial coordinates – it is not a grid, it is a becoming, which may indeed frustrate the colonizing spaces of market orientated mimicry. It might, as such, provide the basis of a relational immune system (RIS) that does not look to perceive of something that exists outside the self as a nonself, but perceives of a 'multiplicity of perceptual worlds'.[53] It is this notion of a RIS that needs more work. Indeed, in contrast to the binary between the phenomenological I and the crowd brains of mass psychology, there needs to be an investigation into these relational bridges that span across multiple perceptual worlds. This might lead to a critical social psychology of the transindividual which invests in care systems designed to lessen the anxiety of transindividuation as well as defending against the horror of marketing contagions intended to surreptitiously piggyback the imitative nature of this relation.

Disclosure statement

No potential conflict of interest was reported by the author.

Notes

[1] Parikka and Sampson, *The Spam Book*, 15, and Sampson, *Virality*, 127–143.
[2] Langlois and Elmer, "The Research Politics of Social Media Platforms."
[3] Ibid., 5.
[4] Nagy, *A History of Modern Immunology*, 241.
[5] Ibid., 241.
[6] Schwartz, "Review of The Immune Self: Theory or Metaphor?"
[7] Parikka and Sampson, *The Spam Book*.
[8] Ibid., 15.
[9] Ibid.
[10] Tarde, *The Laws of Imitation*.
[11] Tarde, *Penal Philosophy*, 116–118.
[12] Caillois, "Mimicry and Legendary Psychasthenia."
[13] Thrift, "Pass It On: Towards a Political Economy of Propensity," and Arvidsson and Malossi, "Customer Co-Production from Social Factory to Brand: Learning from Italian Fashion."
[14] Drenten, "Snapshots of the self: exploring the role of online mobile photo sharing in identity development among adolescent girls," 15.
[15] Ibid., 6.
[16] Ibid., 6.
[17] Deleuze and Guattari, *Anti-Oedipus*, 218–19.
[18] Ibid., 218–19.
[19] Williamson, *Decoding Advertisements: Ideology and Meaning in Advertising*.
[20] Ibid., 63–64.
[21] Ibid., 63.
[22] Ibid., 48.
[23] Ibid., 63.
[24] Caillois, "Mimicry and Legendary Psychasthenia," 24–25.
[25] Jussi Parikka, *Insect Media: An Archaeology of Animals and Technology* (Minneapolis, University of Minnesota Press, 2010), 97.
[26] Ibid., 98.
[27] Ibid., 104.
[28] Ibid., 100.
[29] Caillois, "Mimicry and Legendary Psychasthenia (1936)," 28.
[30] Kramer et al., "Experimental evidence of massive-scale emotional contagion through social networks."
[31] Carr, "The Manipulators: Facebook's Social Engineering Project."
[32] Ibid.
[33] Ibid.
[34] Sampson and Parikka, "Learning from Network Dysfunctionality: Accidents, Enterprise, and Small Worlds of Infection."
[35] Sampson and Parikka, "Learning from Network Dysfunctionality," 457.
[36] Ibid., 457.
[37] Caillois, "Mimicry and Legendary Psychasthenia (1936)," 25.
[38] Ibid.
[39] Parikka, *Insect Media*, 140–44.
[40] Ibid., 141.
[41] Ellis and Tucker, *The Social Psychology of Emotion*, 178.
[42] Ibid., 171–179.
[43] Greenfield, *Everyware: The Dawning Age of Ubiquitous Computing*, 81.
[44] Ibid., 84.
[45] Ibid., 86–87.
[46] Ibid., 86.
[47] Ellis and Tucker, *The Social Psychology of Emotion*, 171.
[48] Ibid., 172.
[49] Ibid., 173.
[50] Ibid., 174.
[51] Ibid., 175.
[52] Ibid., 175.
[53] Ibid., 174

Bibliography

Arvidsson, Adam, and Giannino Malossi. "Customer Co-Production from Social Factory to Brand: Learning from Italian Fashion." In *Inside Marketing: Practices, Ideologies, Devices*, edited by Detlev Zwic and Julien Cayla, Oxford: Oxford University Press, 2011.

Caillois, Roger. "Mimicry and Legendary Psychasthenia (1936)." Translated by John Shepley. *October* 31, (1984): 24–25.

Carr, Nicholas. "The Manipulators: Facebook's Social Engineering Project." *The Los Angeles Review of Books* (September 14, 2014). Accessed September 2016. http://lareviewofbooks.org/essay/manipulators-facebooks-social-engineering-project#

Deleuze, Gilles, and Félix Guattari. *Anti-Oedipus*. London: Athlone Press, 1984.
Drenten, Jenna. "Snapshots of the self: exploring the role of online mobile photo sharing in identity development among adolescent girls." In *Online consumer behavior: theory and research in social media, advertising, and e-tail*, edited by Angeline G Close, New York, NY: Routledge, 2012.
Ellis, Darren, and Ian Tucker. *The Social Psychology of Emotion*. London: Sage, 2015.
Greenfield, Adam. *Everyware: The Dawning Age of Ubiquitous Computing*. New York, NY: New Riders, 2006.
Kramer, Adam D.I. et al. "Experimental evidence of massive-scale emotional contagion through social networks." *Proc Natl Acad Sci USA* 111.24, (2014): 8788–8790. Accessed September 2016. http://www.pnas.org/content/111/24/8788.full
Langlois, Ganaele and Greg Elmer. "The Research Politics of Social Media Platforms." *Culture Machine* 14, (2013). Accessed September 2016. http://www.culturemachine.net/index.php/cm/article/viewArticle/505
Nagy, Zoltan A. *A History of Modern Immunology: The Path Toward Understanding*. New York, NY: Elsevier, 2014.
Parikka, Jussi. *Insect Media: An Archaeology of Animals and Technology*. Minneapolis, MN: University of Minnesota Press, 2010.
Parikka, Jussi, and Tony D. Sampson. *The Spam Book: On Viruses, Porn and Other Anomalies From the Dark Side of Digital Culture*. New Jersey: Hampton, 2009.
Sampson, Tony D. *Virality: Contagion Theory in the Age of Networks*. Minneapolis, MN: Minnesota University Press, 2012.
Sampson, Tony D., and Jussi Parikka. "Learning from Network Dysfunctionality: Accidents, Enterprise, and Small Worlds of Infection." In *A Companion to New Media Dynamics*, edited by John Hartley, Jean Burgess and Axel Bruns, Chichester: John Wiley, 2013.
Schwartz, Robert S. "Review of The Immune Self: Theory or Metaphor?" *New England Journal of Medicine* 332, (1995): 1176-77. Accessed August 2015. http://www.nejm.org/doi/full/10.1056/NEJM199504273321718
Tarde, Gabriel. *Penal Philosophy*. New Jersey: Transactional Publisher, 2001.
Tarde, Gabriel. *The Laws of Imitation*. Translated by E. C. Parsons. New York: Henry Holt, 1903.
Thrift, Nigel. "Pass It On: Towards a Political Economy of Propensity." In *The Social after Tarde: Debates and Assessments*, edited by Matei Candea, London: Routledge, 2010.
Williamson, Judith. *Decoding Advertisements: Ideology and Meaning in Advertising*. London: Marion Boyars, 1978.

Contagion, Virology, Autoimmunity: Derrida's Rhetoric of Contamination

Peta Mitchell

If the theme of this special issue conjures up the name of any single philosopher or cultural theorist, it is that of Derrida, who in the early 1990s began to speak and write of a 'logic of autoimmunity' that at once underpins and internally undermines political, legal and cultural systems such as religion, democracy and the nation-state. As a biopolitical or biophilosophical concept, autoimmunity attaches itself to Derrida, and yet he is certainly not the only philosopher to invoke discourses either of immunology in general or autoimmunity in particular. Indeed, as Inge Mutsaers explains in her recent book on immunological discourse in political philosophy, the discourse of autoimmunity that has emerged over the past quarter century has now 'firmly taken root in political and cultural philosophy' and can be seen not only in the work of Derrida, but also in that of Roberto Esposito, Jean Baudrillard and Byung-Chul Han.[1] Nonetheless, as Mutsaers puts it, among these philosophers, it is Derrida who 'develops autoimmunity into a full political concept'.[2] The point at which autoimmunity enters Derridean discourse in the early to mid 1990s roughly coincides with what has been taken to be Derrida's ethico-political turn, and indeed autoimmunity is often treated as a key signifier of a 'political' shift in Derrida's thinking away from his earlier 'linguistic' concerns with rhetoric, signification, textuality.

Although many scholars have critiqued this notion of a fundamental shift or rupture in Derrida's work (a point to which I'll return) and have similarly claimed that Derrida's rhetorical concerns are evident in his later 'ethico-political' work and vice versa, what I aim to do in this paper is to reveal the tropological line that runs through and connects these concerns. I do this by setting Derrida's later discourse of autoimmunity in the context of what I am calling his ongoing rhetoric of contamination, which I trace from his early use of metaphors of contamination and contact, through to his later deployment of epidemiological and immunological tropes. In doing this, I wish to draw out the always-already contamination of and by rhetoric exemplified in the biophilosophical concept of autoimmunity, which is often critiqued from *outside* philosophy as a metaphor that has been mis- or poorly re-appropriated from the biomedical domain. Given autoimmunity's complex relationship to metaphor – its semantic transference back and forth, across and among juridico-political, biomedical and biophilosophical domains – situating autoimmunity within Derrida's rhetoric of contamination enables a stronger understanding of the rhetorico-political forces at play in the logic of autoimmunity.

Contaminating rhetoric: contamination and/as metaphor

From the very outset, Derrida's oeuvre is tainted with, haunted by, contamination's trace. In the early 1950s, as a second-year student at the École Normale Supérieure, Derrida wrote his first book-length study – a dissertation on Husserl – which remained unpublished until 1990 and which was translated into English in 2003 as *The Problem of Genesis in Husserl's Philosophy*. Although in the body of his dissertation Derrida makes no explicit mention of (the word) contamination, in his preface from 1953/54, the student Derrida remarked on a 'dissimulated contamination' that complicates any notion of an absolute or absolutely pure origin or essence.[3] Looking back on his dissertation in his 1990 preface, Derrida – who, at the time, is on the cusp of his so-called 'political' or 'ethical' turn – appears to seize upon his earlier, almost castaway references to contamination. While chiding his younger self for the 'impudence' of his 'panoramic' and 'scanner'-like reading of Husserl, Derrida notes that this reading nonetheless uncovers and puts into play a 'sort of law' or 'necessity', which 'since then, *even in its literal formulation*, [...] will not have stopped commanding everything I have tried to prove'.[4] Answering his own posed question of 'What necessity?', Derrida continues:

> It is always a question of an originary complication of the origin, of an initial contamination of the simple [...] In fact the question that governs the whole trajectory is already: 'How can the originarity of a foundation be an *a priori* synthesis? How can everything start with a complication?' All the limits on which phenomenological discourse is constructed are examined from the standpoint of the fatal necessity of a 'contamination' ('unperceived entailment or dissimulated contamination' between the two edges of the opposition: transcendental/ 'worldly', eidetic/empirical, intentional/nonintentional, active/passive, present/nonpresent, pointlike/non-pointlike, originary/derived, pure/impure, etc.), the quaking of each border coming to propagate itself onto all the others. A law of differential contamination imposes its logic from one end of the book to the other; and I ask myself why the very word 'contamination' has not stopped imposing itself on me from thence forward.[5]

Despite the fact that Derrida himself calls attention to his ongoing preoccupation both with the concept and the word *contamination*, surprisingly little has been written that engages directly with the question of contamination in and across Derrida's work,[6] and dedicated entries for contamination are noticeably absent from published dictionaries of Derridean terms.[7] By the time Derrida's dissertation was published in 1990, however, Derrida's 'law of differential contamination' can be detected – both implicitly and explicitly – throughout his early critiques of phenomenology and spilling over into his exploration of the problematics of writing and rhetoric from the mid 1960s. It is here, I argue, that Derrida develops a rhetoric of contamination – one that is indistinguishable from this 'law' of contamination; that is figured and enacted through a number of key epidemiological and immunological tropes; and that connects his rhetorical, philosophical and political concerns.

In Derrida's early work on Husserl and phenomenology, *contamination* stands in for or takes the space of a word Derrida states he 'had to give up', namely *dialectic*.[8] As a concept, dialectic cannot adequately address or express the interpenetrating relationship between inside and outside, the failure to keep the origin 'pure' from that which would contaminate it. As Christina Howells explains, in his 1967 *Voice and Phenomenon: Introduction to the Problem of the Sign in Husserl's Phenomenology*, Derrida is not only concerned with how 'Husserl has struggled to show the pure, self-present origin to which extraneous elements such as indication, retention and division or absence are retrospectively added', he also 'argues for a reversal of priorities':

> The additional or 'supplementary' features are in fact nothing of the sort, they are essential to the very constitution that they have been deemed to contaminate. Truth and subjectivity do not exist in a realm prior to language, they depend on language for their very existence. Husserl's desire to preserve the immediacy of presence has been thwarted by the logic of his own arguments: there is no original presence, only representation; no direct intuition, only mediated knowledge; no pure present moment, only a contamination of past and future; no selfidentity, only irremediable self-division and difference.[9]

As such, as Derrida puts it, contamination denotes 'the originary "contamination" of the origin' vis-à-vis phenomenology and indicates the point at which the oppositional logic of dialectic begins to make way for the contaminatory processes of difference, supplement and trace.[10] This linguistic-conceptual shift from *dialectic* to *contamination* doubles back on itself to reveal also the contaminatory relationship between word and concept, language and thought. Philosophy must not only contend with an impure origin or essence, it must also contend with the contaminating force of an impure language.

Derrida's *Writing and Difference* and *Of Grammatology*, both published in 1967, the same year as *Voice and Phenomenon*, display a developing rhetoric of contamination. As Derrida argues in 'Violence and Metaphysics', a 1964 essay on Levinas collected in *Writing and Difference*, phenomenology – and philosophy more broadly – has failed to properly account for language and, specifically, for metaphor. Phenomenological experience cannot be immediate or unmediated by language, for the 'the phenomenon supposes original contamination by the sign'.[11] Levinas's privileging of the phenomenological 'face to face' encounter between self and other 'without intermediary and without communion, neither mediate nor immediate', Derrida maintains,

> cannot possibly be encompassed by philosophical speech without immediately revealing, by philosophy's own light, that philosophy's surface is severely cracked, and that what was taken for its solidity is its rigidity. It could doubtless be shown that it is in the nature of Levinas's writing, at its decisive moments, to move along these cracks, masterfully progressing by negations, and by negation against negation. Its proper route is not that of an 'either this ... or that,' but of a 'neither this ... nor that'. The poetic force of metaphor is often the trace of this rejected alternative, this wounding of language. Through it, in its opening, experience itself is silently revealed.[12]

This question of language, of signification, communication and contamination is at base a question of metaphor. Indeed, as Derrida is at pains to point out, the word *phenomenon* is shot through with solar metaphors, the philosophy of phenomenology 'struck with light',[13] even while it tries to erase, suture over its fundamental metaphoricity via a metaphysics of presence. 'Empiricism' – and phenomenology as a form of empiricism – is, Derrida writes, 'thinking *by* metaphor without thinking the metaphor *as such*'.[14]

Indeed, for Derrida, this negation and sublimation of metaphor is at the centre of Western philosophy's quest for an essence via metaphysics, and he explores this question more fully in his 1971 essay 'White Mythology: Metaphor in the Text of Philosophy'. Philosophy, as metaphysics, Derrida argues, is predicated upon the idea of a knowable truth or essence that may be expressed or 'got at' via a direct, literal language. Metaphor – by saying something is what it is not – not only constitutes a 'detour' that threatens not to return to the proper, but also takes the form of the *pharmakon*, a dangerous 'supplementary' language that contaminates and undermines proper language and reasoning. Metaphysics, according to Derrida is, put simply, just that: a 'white mythology' that 'assembles and reflects Western culture'.[15] This mythology is built upon a central foundational, yet self-effacing metaphor: the metaphor of the sun. Although Western philosophy, as metaphysics, has drawn much of its power from this foundational solar metaphor, to assert itself as logos and reason it must attempt to erase its mythical foundations, 'erase within itself', Derrida writes, 'the fabulous scene that has produced it'.[16] As I have written elsewhere, that 'fabulous scene' that lies stirring just beneath philosophy's surface is figurative language – a supposedly supplementary language, 'a "detour" or deviance that must be reappropriated by proper or literal language'.[17]

As Derrida explains in 'White Mythology', philosophy considers metaphor to be 'a provisional loss of meaning, a form of economy that does no irreparable damage to what is proper, an inevitable detour', but one that falls 'within the horizon of a circular reappropriation of the proper sense'.[18] And yet, metaphor is dangerous to philosophy because it always threatens not to return to the proper: metaphor is both '*mimesis* trying its chance, *mimesis* at risk', always threatening to 'fail to attain truth', and as such 'must reckon with a definite absence'.[19] At the same time, the proper – the language of essence – cannot itself be immune to linguistic contamination.[20] Thus, Derrida enjoins us to 'dismantle' and 'reconstitute' the 'metaphysical and rhetorical structures' at work in philosophy so that we may 'begin to identify the historical terrain–the problematic–in which it has been possible to inquire systematically of philosophy the metaphorical credentials of its concepts'.[21] In short, this is the task and purpose of what he calls a 'general "metaphorology"'.[22]

By the time Derrida publishes *Dissemination* the following year (1972), the question of metaphor and the question of contamination have been brought into the same frame: 'metaphoricity' becomes, as I have quoted above, 'the logic of contamination and the contamination of logic'.[23] In *Of Grammatology*, Derrida had already taken Saussure to task for attempting – not unlike Plato in the *Phaedrus* – to cast writing as 'the most perfidious, most permanent contamination which has not ceased to menace, even to corrupt' the 'purity' of speech.[24] Saussure's 'vehement argumentation' against this supposed 'contamination by writing', Derrida continues, 'aims at more than a theoretical error, more than a moral fault: at a sort of stain and primarily at a sin'.[25] In returning to Plato's speech/writing dichotomy in *Dissemination*, Derrida argues that, like writing, metaphor is portrayed a dangerous supplement, a *pharmakon*, a parasite, a contaminant. It is, as he puts it in a later essay, a 'bad' *mimesis* that 'haunts' or 'contaminates' good *mimesis*.[26]

Derrida perhaps comes closest to articulating explicitly *why* contamination offers itself as a strategic metaphor *for* metaphor in yet another essay on Levinas, his 'At This Very Moment in This Work Here I Am', published in 1980. Here, Derrida pronounces that Levinas 'detests contamination', and yet 'what holds his writing in suspense is that one must welcome contamination, the *risk* of contamination'.[27] The discourse of contamination that he is 'enchaining', Derrida explains some pages later,

> Usually […] implies a stain or poisoning by the contagion of some improper body. Here simple contact suffices, since it will have interrupted the interruption. Contact would be a priori contaminating. Graver yet, the risk of contamination would surface *before* there is contact, in the simple *necessity of tying* together interruptions as such, in the very seriality of traces and the insistence of the ruptures. And even if this unheard-of chain does not retie threads but hiatuses. Contamination then is no longer a risk but a fate that must be assumed. The knots in the series contaminate without contact, as if the two edges re-established continuity at a distance by the simple vis-à-vis of

> their lines. Still, it is no longer a matter of edges, since there is no longer any line, only tapering points absolutely disjointed from one shore to the other of the interruption.[28]

Contamination, contact, contagion. From this point, the words go hand-in-hand. In 'On Reading Heidegger', an outline of Derrida's remarks to a 1986 colloquium, he defines contamination as 'a contagion born of contact and a kind of touching [that] foils every strategy of protection'.[29] What 'scares' Heidegger, according to Derrida is the '*contamination* between touching and nontouching', the 'contamination between touching in the human sense and touching in the nonhuman sense, technical, animal, or whatever'.[30] It is perhaps not surprising that these words begin to constellate around one another in Derrida's writing of the 1980s. Certainly, the etymology of contamination is not unlike that of contagion. Both words stem from the Latin *tangere*, meaning 'to touch', and both terms carry overtones of tainting, colouring, corruption, infection or pollution caused by a form of touching together or admixture.[31] Moreover, the philological meaning of contamination is highly pertinent to considering Derrida's rhetoric of contamination. In philology the term contamination refers to a 'blending of forms, words, or phrases of similar meaning or use so as to produce a form, word, or phrase of a new type'.[32]

Contamination, in this sense, is creative, bringing about a new linguistic form through blending. Similarly, in Derrida's formulation, contamination is also not simply de-structive; rather, it reveals the workings of *différance*. Contamination, Derrida explains, is not as Heidegger would 'insist [...] merely an "ontic" scheme, a mere "metaphor"', but instead 'requires the thinking of a kind of *différance* that is not yet or no longer ontological difference'.[33] Deployed against philosophy's submerged or elided metaphors of enlightenment and purity, contamination exposes the necessary *différance* at its core – contamination conveys, in a single word, the 'menace of supplementarity, parasitism, technique'.[34] For Geoffrey Bennington, the 'metonymic contamination' that *différance* engenders is 'not at all an interiority closed in upon itself', but rather an 'opening'.[35] The 'necessity of contamination' is an affirmation, it is itself what 'deconstruction affirms, what it says "yes, yes" to'.[36] Derrida himself registers the affirmatory nature of contamination in a 1994 interview, published as 'Nietzsche and the Machine'. 'One should not', Derrida states in this interview, 'simply consider contamination as a threat'. Contamination must always be 'assumed' and 'affirmed' not only because 'it is also opening or chance, our chance' but also because 'it is the very possibility of affirmation in the first place'.[37] 'So you see', Derrida concludes, 'in fact, nothing can be simple, and contamination is a good thing!'[38]

By the late 1980s, Derrida's rhetoric of contamination has encompassed not only contagion and parasitism, but also virality and infection. Rhetoric itself, Derrida argues (perhaps tellingly, in a supplementary note) is 'a parasitic or viral structure: in its origins and in general'.[39] Invoking computer viruses and AIDS, he asks, 'whether viewed from up close or from far away, does not everything that comes to affect the proper have the form of a virus (neither alive nor dead, neither human nor "reappropriable by the proper of man", nor generally subjectivable)? And doesn't rhetoric always obey a logic of parasitism? Or rather, doesn't the parasite logically and normally disrupt logic?'.[40] In an interview the following year titled 'The Spatial Arts', Derrida draws virality even more strongly into the foreground of his rhetoric of contamination. Again referencing the 'intersection between AIDS and the computer virus', Derrida argues that

> All I have done, to summarize it very reductively, is dominated by the thought of a virus, what could be called a parasitology, a virology, the virus being many things. [...] The virus is in part a parasite that destroys, that introduces disorder into communication. Even from the biological standpoint, this is what happens with a virus; it derails a mechanism of the communicational type, its coding and decoding. On the other hand, it is something that is neither living nor nonliving; the virus is not a microbe. And if you follow these two threads, that of a parasite which disrupts destination from the communicative point of view–disrupting writing, inscription, and the coding and decoding of inscription–and which on the other hand is neither alive nor dead, you have the matrix of all that I have done since I began writing.[41]

This accretion of contagious and contaminatory metaphors in Derridean discourse goes beyond, as I have argued elsewhere, 'mere' metaphor. For Derrida, 'the viral rhetoric of the network age has exploded the possibility of any neat separation between the metaphorical and the proper', making the question of metaphor ever more relevant.[42]

Contamination, the law and violence: towards a law of contamination

By the late 1970s, contamination had, for Derrida, hardened into a 'law' as well as into a conceptual apparatus for understanding the problem of law itself. The 'law of differential contamination' that Derrida, in 1990, identifies in his dissertation on Husserl, appears also in his 1977 essay 'Limited Inc a b c', in which he refers to 'a law of undecidable contamination, which has interested me for some time'.[43] In 'The Law of Genre', first published in 1980, Derrida turns his attention to the ways in which genre – both in its literary and broader classificatory senses – inscribes a particular law that, while attempting to quarantine itself from impurity or mixture, is founded upon a principle of contamination. '[A]s soon as genre announces itself', Derrida writes, 'one must respect a norm, one must not cross a line of demarcation, one must not risk impurity, anomaly, or monstrosity'.[44] And yet, he asks,

> What if there were, lodged within the heart of the law itself, a law of impurity or a principle of contamination? And suppose

> the condition for the possibility of the law were the *a priori* of a counter-law, an axiom of impossibility that would confound its sense, order, and reason?[45]

Genre's boundaries are continually and always-already pervaded by external 'disruptive "anomalies"', such as repetition, citation and re-citation – a disruption for which Derrida provides a number of alternative names: 'Impurity, corruption, contamination, decomposition, perversion, deformation, even cancerisation, generous proliferation, or degenerescence'.[46] Yet again, however, contamination remains the privileged term. If the law of genre were itself governed by a law, Derrida concludes, this 'law of the law of genre' would be 'precisely a principle of contamination, a law of impurity, a parasitical economy'.[47]

Where Derrida engages most directly with law and with the law of contamination, however, is in his monumental essay of 1989, 'Force of Law', which was originally presented as a seminar at the Cardozo Law School. It is here that we see the rhetoric of contamination entering into and engaging with legal discourse. In 'Force of Law', Derrida takes up the question of Law's purity and autonomy – what he calls the '"mystical foundation" of authority', approaching the question via Walter Benjamin's 'Critique of Violence'. If we were to identify the single most influential foundational, yet self-effacing, metaphor for Law, it must be Hans Kelsen's notion of a closed system of 'pure' law. In his *Pure Theory of Law*, first published in German in 1934, Kelsen sought to carve out a defined, autonomous space for Law by separating it from contaminating external influences, such as psychology, sociology, ethics and political theory, and by positing a *grundnorm,* or basic norm, upon which all other norms might be founded. It would be convenient if Kelsen had used the term 'contaminating' – as I just did – to describe the outside influences affecting the purity and autonomy of Law's borders, but I should be careful to point out he did not. Kelsen does not dwell on the context and philosophical background for his Pure Theory, which is confined to one paragraph at the text's outset in which he rails against the way in which law has been 'adulterated' through its 'uncritical mixing' with other disciplines.[48] The original German terms Kelsen uses to describe the 'adulteration' of Law by other disciplines stem from the word *vermengung*, which translates as 'mixing'. Kelsen notably does not use terms such as the German *kontamination* or *verunreinigung*, meaning pollution or contamination, and yet *vermengung* does retain that particular philological sense of *contamination* – of linguistic blending – pointed out earlier.

Unlike and against Kelsen, who posits the legal fiction of the *grundnorm* in order to provide a cornerstone for Law's authority and autonomy, Derrida argues that law's authority is built upon the act of sovereign violence – an act that at once founds law and conserves it, an act that is both originary and conservatory in its endless iterability, and one that cannot be reduced to a norm. There is, he maintains, 'no more a pure foundation or a pure position of law, and so a pure founding violence, than there is a purely conservative violence'.[49] In place of a norm, then, can only be found what Derrida calls 'a *différantielle* contamination' between law's creation and conservation, 'with all the paradoxes that this may lead to'.[50] This, too, is connected with Derrida's theory of language, and particularly figurative language. As Petra Gehring has pointed out, in 'Force of Law', Derrida maintains that

> if the pure means disavows itself in language, which cannot deny its 'mystical foundation', then the hope of a breach with the 'mystical foundation of the authority' of law is also disavowed. [...] Law admits no pure solutions, no good decisions, and in this sense it must admit to being violent just as, according to Derrida, language–everything in which mediation is somehow at work–is necessarily 'contaminated'.[51]

As such, Derridean contamination must deny or at the very least problematize the kind of autonomy posited for law both by Kelsen's purity thesis and also, more recently by Niklas Luhmann and Gunther Teubner's autopoietic theories of law.[52] Margaret Davies has, in some detail, discussed the ways in which Derrida's law of impurity or contamination complexifies and is complexified by Kelsen's pure theory of law. If, she says, we take the basic norm not simply to be the 'foundation for the legal system, but rather a rupture or limit which makes the legal system possible', Kelsen's purity thesis, which is 'wholly reliant on self-legitimation through *exclusion* of an other, at this point *becomes* the other: the inside and the outside are undecidable, and we have a limit of impurity'.[53] Impurity becomes, according to Davies a law in itself: it marks every law with its stain and becomes the very 'condition for the claim of purity'. [54]

The law of contamination and the logic of autoimmunity

In Derrida's later work, his law of contamination or impurity – with its attendant metaphors of contagion, infection and virology – begins to make way for a logic of autoimmunity, and as I established at the outset of this essay, Derrida's shift towards immunological tropes in the 1990s are often considered a primary marker of his ethico-political turn. Of course, Derrida himself rejected suggestions that his work could be divided up, parceled out into neat, well-bounded categories, 'shifts' or 'turns'; for this drive to classify, categorize and draw boundaries must, like any other, be subject to the same principle of contamination that underpins the deconstructive endeavour. Although, as Maebh Long has put it, this 'contamination' within and among the phases of Derrida's writing needs to be acknowledged, an ethico-political 'shift in Derrida's texts is nonetheless generally recognised', a shift that is in many respects marked by the entrance of autoimmunity.[55]

In mapping out the emergence of Derrida's concept of autoimmunity, Elizabeth Rottenberg notes that a 'general logic of "autoimmunity"' can be traced to his 1996 essay 'Faith and Knowledge', even though the term *autoimmunity* appears in Derrida's writing for the first time some years earlier in *Specters of Marx* (1993) and *Politics of Friendship* (1994).[56] In *Specters*, Derrida invokes the law of contamination when he describes 'the essential contamination of spirit (*Geist*) by specter (*Gespenst*)' and later employs *contamination* as a byword for haunting of and by the other.[57] Derrida's reference to autoimmunity in *Specters* is equally brief, but nonetheless is framed in terms strongly reminiscent of his earlier rhetoric of contamination and suggestive of the ways his future interest in autoimmunity will develop. 'The living ego', Derrida writes in *Specters*, 'is auto-immune':

> To protect its life, to constitute itself as unique living ego, to relate, as the same, to itself it is necessarily led to welcome the other within (so many figures of death: differance of the technical apparatus, iterability, non-uniqueness, prosthesis, synthetic image, simulacrum, all of which begins with language, before language), it must therefore take the immune defenses apparently meant for the non-ego, the enemy, the opposite, the adversary and direct them at once *for itself and against itself*.[58]

Autoimmunity seems here to take Derrida's logic of contamination one step further. Where to this point Derrida has deployed a rhetoric of contamination in order to maintain that an essence cannot remain pure and untainted by that which it would define as impure or exterior to it (that is, the self or essence is always-already contaminated by the other), autoimmunity suggests the contamination of the self by the self *as* other, such that self and non-self can no longer simply be recognized. A few years later, Derrida would make autoimmunity a guiding motif in his analysis of religion in the essay 'Faith and Knowledge'. Here Derrida declares a 'general logic of auto-immunisation' that he would extend further in the context of terrorism in his 2001 interview 'Autoimmunity: Real and Symbolic Suicides' and further again in the context of sovereignty and the nation-state in *Rogues*, published in 2003.

Viewed in this way, there is an apparent – if apparently superficial – shift to the political in the linear-temporal mapping that I have performed: from philosophical to rhetorical concerns and thence to law and religion, and on to terror, sovereignty and the nation-state. In her essay on autoimmunity, Long describes the lengths to which Derrida went in order to articulate, retrospectively, the continuity of the political throughout his writing, to smooth over what had been portrayed as a rupture in his *oeuvre*. Rather than existing as self-contained systems laid out along a developmental line of progress, Derrida's texts, according to Long,

> operate in ironic, aphoristic relation to each other, each a foreword and an epilogue to another, each a reengagement and a rewriting, independent and conjoined. Each text is in counterpoint with every other text, in time and out of time. Each new text changes every other text, always a preface to a further fragment'.[59]

This observation presupposes also a double-movement – just as Derrida's seemingly non- or pre-political works can be seen to be contaminated with the same preoccupations as his 'political' ones, so too can his 'political' works be seen to be contaminated with the same concerns as his philosophical and rhetorical ones. And this double movement is nowhere more apparent than in the figure of autoimmunity, which raises again questions of rhetoric and metaphor.

In their recent work of medical history, *Intolerant Bodies: A Short History of Autoimmunity*, Warwick Anderson and Ian R. Mackay are mildly disparaging of Derrida's philosophical cooptation of the biomedical term *autoimmunity*. Derrida, portrayed as a 'roguish' philosopher with 'admirers' rather than interlocutors, is described as 'discover[ing] autoimmunity in the early 1990s' and becoming 'obsessed' with it, notwithstanding the at-times 'eccentric' nature of his 'understanding of autoimmune pathology'.[60] A hint of equivocation also attends their assessment of philosophers, such as Derrida and Roberto Esposito, who have been 'gripped' by the 'allure' of autoimmunity: 'Their history may be unreliable, their findings belated', Anderson and Mackay write,

> but one has to admire the fervor that infuses their proclamation of the significance of immunity for our discernment of self and other, for our appreciation of security and danger, for the understanding of life and its contrary. In the twenty-first century, immunology–autoimmunity especially–seems applicable everywhere.[61]

One senses that, although autoimmunity 'seems applicable everywhere', Anderson and Mackay would prefer that it did not, or that at least it was not 'deploy[ed] with abandon' in Derridean fashion.[62] What appears to make Anderson and Mackay uncomfortable is the trafficking of metaphors across and between the domains of science and philosophy, and to be fair, their concern goes in both directions. They acknowledge immunity's origins in the social domain – a point that I will return to – and that philosophy's adoption of autoimmunity represented, in some respects, immunity's 'returning [...] from whence it came'.[63] Nevertheless, they raise concerns about the potential for conceptual contamination and corruption *in both directions* as a result of 'metaphoric borrowing'.[64]

In 'Faith and Knowledge', Derrida calls attention to immunity's grounding in the juridico-political realm. In Roman society, to be *immunis* meant to be exempt from service (*munis*) and from the charges, taxes or obligations (*munera*) rendered to benefit the *communis* or community. As Derrida notes, this concept of immunity as a 'freedom' or 'exception' from service or obligation 'was subsequently transported into the domains of constitutional or international law (parliamentary or diplomatic immunity), but it also belongs to the history of the Christian Church and to canon law'.[65] In *A Body Worth Defending: Immunity, Biopolitics, and the Apotheosis of the Modern Body*, Ed Cohen provides a detailed and insightful overview of immunity's etymology and history as a concept, pointedly noting that the 'legal concept [of immunity] predates its biomedical appropriation by at least two thousand years'.[66] Science's metaphorization of immunity must be taken seriously, Cohen argues, because 'we need to appreciate much more palpably the imaginary work that metaphor performs in and as science'[67] – or, in Derridean terms, we need to acknowledge the 'fabulous scene' that underpins science as well as philosophy. Additionally, as Michael M. J. Fischer has cautioned, we need to better understand how metaphorical usages within science writing are not simply fixed, dead metaphors or 'premature closures' of meaning. Rather, Fischer maintains, metaphors in the body of science are '*pointers* to fields of difference or terms within a series or cascade of signifiers. Science never stops its mapping, its drilling down, and as knowledge changes, so too do high-level metaphors'.[68]

In consciously engaging with the question of metaphor and scientificity, Derrida, according to Cohen, 'proposes a new interplay between epistemological and metaphorical effects by reanimating the living metaphor in bioscience'.[69] Philosophy's appropriation of immunity is, therefore, a reappropriation; it is not simply a metaphorization, but a remetaphorization, resulting in what might be thought of as a 'biopolitical hybrid'.[70] W. J. T. Mitchell makes a similar point in his essay on Derrida's application of autoimmune logic to terrorism in the aftermath of 9/11. 'The whole theory of the immune system and the discipline of immunology', Mitchell writes,

> is riddled with images drawn from the sociopolitical sphere–of invaders and defenders, hosts and parasites, natives and aliens, and of borders and identities that must be maintained. In asking us to see terror as autoimmunity, then, Derrida is bringing the metaphor home at the same time he sends it abroad, stretching it to the limits of the world. The effect of the bipolar image, then, is to produce a situation in which there is *no literal meaning*, nothing but the resonances between two images, one bio-medical, the other political.[71]

Immunity therefore has a semantic porosity – one that is mirrored in the body its biomedical sense assumes. As Michael Lewis explains, although the immune system establishes a boundary between the self and non-self in order to 'protect the identity of the vital substance', it is a permeable and 'porous and shifting' boundary that must allow 'a certain measure of alterity (otherness) [to be] incorporated into the very identity (sameness) of the organism and installed as an essential part of the protective apparatus itself, as if one could not protect the identity of the self without incorporating a measure of otherness within it'.[72] Immunity's slippage back and forth across domains, its assumption of porous and fundamentally permeable boundaries, and its necessary confusion of self and other presuppose both a rhetoric *and* a logic of contamination.

Autoimmunity further complicates this by introducing into the equation a perverse – in Derrida's terms 'quasi-suicidal'[73] – drive, one that 'amounts to the self's attacking its own organs, tissues and processes, including the very immune system which was to have protected it and its identity'.[74] As Derrida explains in 'Faith and Knowledge', any attempt to essentialize, to delimit and isolate an essence in its purity (whether it be religion, law, or philosophy) is thwarted by its predicates or supplements, which cannot simply be hived off. In any given case, he explains, 'there are at least *two* families, two strata or sources that overlap, mingle, contaminate each another without ever merging; and just in case things are still too simple, one of the two is precisely the drive to remain unscathed, on the part of that which is allergic to contamination, *save by itself, auto-immunely*'.[75] In other words, what autoimmunity serves to thematize is the drive that always-already and perversely counters *from within* the overlapping drive to remain uncontaminated, unscathed, *heilig*. Autoimmunity in this sense, then, reveals itself as the limit of the law of contamination – indeed as the contamination of contamination.

Notes

[1] Mutsaers, *Immunological Discourse in Political Philosophy*, 95.
[2] Ibid., 96.
[3] Derrida, *The Problem of Genesis in Husserl's Philosophy*, xl.
[4] Ibid., xiv, emphasis in original.
[5] Ibid., xv. With his reference to "unperceived entailment or dissimulated contamination," Derrida is quoting from the preface of his original dissertation.
[6] Cf. Arkady Plotnitsky's essay on the violence presupposed by Derridean contamination, along with Douglas L. Donkel's examination of the relationship between différance and contamination, Andrew Mitchell's investigation of Derrida's concept of contamination in relation to Heidegger, and Beata Stawarska's reading of Derrida and Saussure on contamination and entrainment are notable exceptions.
[7] See Niall Lucy's *A Derrida Dictionary*, Simon Morgan Wortham's *The Derrida Dictionary*, and Maria-Daniella Dick and Julian Wolfreys's *Derrida Wordbook*. Although none of these texts provides a dedicated entry for 'contamination', the word does, however, appear a number of times in each, and, in the *Derrida Wordbook*, most notably in the entry devoted to "Virus."
[8] Derrida, *The Problem of Genesis in Husserl's Philosophy*, xv.
[9] Howells, *Deconstruction from Phenomenology to Ethics*, 38.
[10] Derrida, *The Problem of Genesis in Husserl's Philosophy*, xv. See also Leonard Lawlor, who notes that the word 'dialectic' is 'virtually absent in Derrida's "Violence and Metaphysics" [...] and in *Voice and Phenomena*, and, by the time of "The Ends of Man" in 1968, it will have completely disappeared from Derrida's lexicon of positive terms. Instead, the words "undecidability," "contamination," and, of course, "différance" will replace it'. See Lawlor, *Derrida and Husserl*, 140.
[11] Derrida, "Violence and Metaphysics," 161.
[12] Ibid., 112.
[13] Ibid., 104. The word phenomenology, as John McCumber explains, is 'composed of two Greek words "phenomenon" and "logos" [...] The Greek phainomenon, for its part, has a good deal of structure: it is the present neuter middle participle of phainein, meaning to shine, show or bring to light. In the middle voice, this means to bring oneself to light, or to show oneself; and as a neuter participle, it refers to the action of doing this on the part of a thing. A "phenomenon" is thus something that brings itself to light as a thing'. See McCumber, *Time and Philosophy*, 162.
[14] Derrida, "Violence and Metaphysics," 174.
[15] Derrida, "White Mythology: Metaphor in the Text of Philosophy," 11.
[16] Ibid., 11.
[17] Mitchell, *Cartographic Strategies of Postmodernity*, 11.

[18] Derrida, "White Mythology," 73.
[19] Ibid., 42.
[20] Ibid., 48.
[21] Ibid., 13.
[22] Ibid., 18.
[23] Derrida, *Dissemination*, 149.
[24] Derrida, *Of Grammatology*, 34.
[25] Ibid.
[26] Derrida, "Rhetoric of Drugs," 7.
[27] Derrida, "At This Very Moment," 162.
[28] Ibid., 167.
[29] Derrida, "On Reading Heidegger," 171.
[30] Ibid., 177–178, emphasis in original.
[31] See also Derrida's *On Touching–Jean-Luc Nancy*, first published in 2000, in which he explores the relationship between contamination, contact, and the figure of touch. See Derrida, *On Touching*, 75, 109.
[32] "Contamination," *OED online*.
[33] Derrida, "On Reading Heidegger," 172.
[34] Ibid., 171.
[35] Bennington and Derrida, *Jacques Derrida*, 73–74.
[36] Ibid., 310.
[37] Derrida, "Nietzsche and the Machine," 56.
[38] Ibid., 64.
[39] Derrida, "Rhetoric of Drugs," 23.
[40] Ibid., 23.
[41] Derrida, "The Spatial Arts," 12.
[42] Mitchell, *Contagious Metaphor*, 139.
[43] Derrida, "Limited Inc a b c," 59.
[44] Derrida, "The Law of Genre," 57.
[45] Ibid., 57.
[46] Derrida, "The Law of Genre," 57–58. See also "Limited Inc," in which Derrida also discusses repetition and iterability in terms of a process of contamination and a parasitic logic that ceaselessly undermines essentializing thought: 'Iterability blurs a priori the dividing-line that passes between [...] opposed terms, "corrupting" it if you like, contaminating it parasitically, qua limit. What is re-markable about the mark includes the margin within the mark. The line delineating the margin can therefore never be determined rigorously, it is never pure and simple'. "Limited Inc," 70. Similarly, in a 1989 interview published as "This Strange Institution Called Literature," Derrida explains that in the formation of an event, 'What happens is always some contamination. The uniqueness of the event is this coming about of a singular relation between the unique and its repetition, its iterability. The event comes about, or promises itself initially, only by thus compromising itself by the singular contamination of the singular and what shares it. It comes about as impurity–and impurity here is chance'. Derrida, "This Strange Institution Called Literature," 68–69.
[47] Derrida, "The Law of Genre," 59.
[48] Kelsen, *Pure Theory of Law*, 1.
[49] Derrida, "Force of Law," 997.
[50] Ibid.
[51] Ibid., 159.
[52] See, for instance, Teubner's edited collection *Autopoietic Law* (1987), which contains Luhmann's essay "The Unity of the Legal System," and Luhmann's *Law as a Social System* (trans. of *Das Recht der Gesellschaft*, 1993).
[53] Davies, "Derrida and Law: Legitimate Fictions," 221.
[54] Ibid.
[55] Long, "Derrida Interviewing Derrida: Autoimmunity and the Laws of the Interview," 106.
[56] Rottenberg, "The Legacy of Autoimmunity," 3.
[57] Derrida, *Specters of Marx*, 141, 201.
[58] Ibid., 177, emphasis in original.
[59] Long, "Derrida Interviewing Derrida," 107.
[60] Anderson and Mackay, *Intolerant Bodies*, 149–150.
[61] Ibid.
[62] Ibid., 146.
[63] Ibid., 144.
[64] Ibid., 145.
[65] Derrida, "Faith and Knowledge," 80, n. 27.
[66] Cohen, *A Body Worth Defending*, 35.
[67] Ibid., 36.
[68] Fischer, "On Metaphor: Reciprocity and Immunity," 149–50. Fischer does, however, suggest that the 'self–nonself' metaphor that accompanied and subtended the biomedical concept of autoimmunity has, within scientific writing 'run its course'.
[69] Cohen, *A Body Worth Defending*, 36–37.
[70] Ibid., 38, 40.
[71] W. J. T. Mitchell, "Picturing Terror: Derrida's Autoimmunity," 282.
[72] Lewis, "Of (Auto-)Immune Life: Derrida, Esposito, Agamben," 215.
[73] Derrida "Autoimmunity," 124.
[74] Lewis, "Of (Auto-)Immune Life: Derrida, Esposito, Agamben," 216.
[75] Derrida, "Faith and Knowledge," 63, emphasis in original.

ORCID

Peta Mitchell http://orcid.org/0000-0003-4523-6685

Bibliography

Anderson, Warwick, and Ian R. Mackay. *Intolerant Bodies: A Short History of Autoimmunity*. Baltimore: Johns Hopkins University Press, 2014.

Bennington, Geoffrey, and Jacques Derrida. *Jacques Derrida*. Chicago: University of Chicago Press, 1993.

Cohen, Ed. *A Body Worth Defending: Immunity, Biopolitics, and the Apotheosis of the Modern Body*. Durham: Duke University Press, 2009.

"Contamination, n." *OED Online*. June 2016. Oxford University Press. http://www.oed.com/view/Entry/40057?redirectedFrom=contamination.

Davies, Margaret. "Derrida and Law: Legitimate Fictions." In *Jacques Derrida and the Humanities*, edited by Tom Cohen, 213–237. Cambridge: Cambridge University Press, 2001.

Derrida, Jacques. "At This Very Moment in This Work Here I Am." In *Psyche: Inventions of the Other*. vol. I, edited by Peggy Kamuf and Elizabeth Rottenberg, 143–190. Stanford: Stanford University Press, 2007.

Derrida, Jacques. "Autoimmunity: Real and Symbolic Suicides–a Dialogue with Jacques Derrida." In *Philosophy in a Time of Terror: Dialogues with Jürgen Habermas and Jacques Derrida*, edited by Giovanna Borradori, 85–136. Chicago, IL: University of Chicago Press, 2003.

Derrida, Jacques. *Dissemination*. Translated by Barbara Johnson. London: Athlone, 1981. Translation of La dissémination, Paris: Éditions du Seuil, 1972.

Derrida, Jacques. "Faith and Knowledge: The Two Sources of 'Religion' at the Limits of Reason Alone [1996]." Translated by Samuel Weber. In *Acts of Religion* edited by Gil Anidjar, 42–101. New York: Routledge, 2002.

Derrida, Jacques. "Force of Law: The 'Mystical Foundation of Authority'." *Cardozo Law Review* 11 (1990): 920–1045.

Derrida, Jacques. "The Law of Genre." Translated by Avital Ronal. *Critical Inquiry* 7, no. 1 (1980): 55–81.

Derrida, Jacques. "Limited Inc a b c..." Translated by Samuel Weber. In *Limited Inc*, 29–110. Evanston, IL: Northwestern University Press, 1988.

Derrida, Jacques. "Nietzsche and the Machine (Interview with Richard Beardsworth)." *Journal of Nietzsche Studies* 7 (1994): 7–66.

Derrida, Jacques. *Of Grammatology*. Translated by Gayatri Chakravorty Spivak. Baltimore: Johns Hopkins University Press, 1997.

Derrida, Jacques. "On Reading Heidegger: An Outline of Remarks to the Essex Colloquium." *Research in Phenomenology* 17 (1987): 171–188.

Derrida, Jacques. *On Touching—Jean-Luc Nancy*. Translated by Christine Irizarry. Stanford: Stanford University Press, 2005.

Derrida, Jacques. *The Problem of Genesis in Husserl's Philosophy*. Translated by Marian Hobson. Chicago: University of Chicago Press, 2002.

Derrida, Jacques. "The Rhetoric of Drugs: An Interview." Translated by Michael Israel. *Differences* 5, no. 1 (1993): 1–25.

Derrida, Jacques. *Rogues: Two Essays on Reason*. Trans. Pascale-Anne Brault and Michael Naas. Stanford: Stanford University Press, 2005.

Derrida, Jacques. "The Spatial Arts: An Interview with Jacques Derrida [1990]." Trans. Laurie Volpe. In *Deconstruction and the Visual Arts* edited by Peter Brunette and David Wills, 9–32. Cambridge: Cambridge University Press, 1994.

Derrida, Jacques. *Specters of Marx*. Translated by Peggy Kamuf. Abingdon: Routledge, 1994. Translation of Spectres de Marx, Paris: Éditions Galileé, 1993.

Derrida, Jacques. "This Strange Institution Called Literature: An Interview with Jacques Derrida [1989]." Translated by Geoffrey Bennington and Rachel Bowlby. In *Acts of Literature* edited by Derek Attridge, 33–75. New York: Routledge, 1992.

Derrida, Jacques. "Violence and Metaphysics." Translated by Alan Bass. In *Writing and Difference*, 97–192. London: Routledge, 2001.

Derrida, Jacques. *Voice and Phenomenon: Introduction to the Problem of the Sign in Husserl's Phenomenology*. Translated by Leonard Lawlor. Evanston, IL: Northwestern University Press, 2011.

Derrida, Jacques. "White Mythology: Metaphor in the Text of Philosophy." Trans. F. C. T. Moore. *New Literary History* 6, no. 1 (1982): 5–74.

Derrida, Jacques. *Writing and Difference*. Translated by Alan Bass. London: Routledge, 2001.

Dick, Maria-Daniella, and Julian Wolfreys. *The Derrida Wordbook*. Edinburgh: Edinburgh University Press, 2013.

Donkel, Douglas L. "Formal Contamination: A Reading of Derrida's Argument." *Philosophy Today* 40, no. 2 (1996): 301–309.

Fischer, Michael M. J. "On Metaphor: Reciprocity and Immunity." *Cultural Anthropology* 27.1 (2012): 144–152.

Gehring, Petra. "Force and the 'Mystical Foundation' of Law: How Jacques Derrida Addresses Legal Discourse." *German Law Journal* 6, no. 1 (2005): 151–169.

Howells, Christina. *Deconstruction from Phenomenology to Ethics*. Cambridge: Polity, 1999.

Kelsen, Hans. *Pure Theory, and of Law*. Trans. Max Knight. Berkeley: University of California Press, 1967. Translation of Reine Rechtslehre, . Vienna: Franz Deuticke, 1934.

Lawlor, Leonard. *Derrida and Husserl: The Basic Problem of Phenomenology*. Bloomington, IN: Indiana University Press, 2002.

Lewis, Michael. "Of (Auto-)Immune Life: Derrida, Esposito, Agamben." In *Medicine and Society, New Perspectives in Continental Philosophy*, edited by Darian Meacham, 213–231. Dordrecht: Springer, 2015.

Long, Maebh. "Derrida Interviewing Derrida: Autoimmunity and the Laws of the Interview." *Australian Humanities Review* 65 (2013): 103–119.

Lucy, Niall. *A Derrida Dictionary*. Malden, MA: Blackwell, 2004.

Luhmann, Niklas. *Law as a Social System*. Translated by Klaus A. Ziegert. Oxford: Oxford University Press, 2004.

McCumber, John. *Time and Philosophy: A History of Continental Thought*. Abingdon: Routledge, 2014.

Mitchell, Andrew. "Contamination, Essence, and Decomposition: Heidegger and Derrida." In *French Interpretations of Heidegger: An Exceptional Reception*, edited by David Pettigrew and François Raffoul, 131–150. Albany: State University of New York Press, 2008.

Mitchell, Peta. *Cartographic Strategies of Postmodernity: The Figure of the Map in Contemporary Theory and Fiction*. New York, NY: Routledge, 2008.

Mitchell, Peta. *Contagious Metaphor*. London: Bloomsbury Academic, 2012.

Mitchell, W. J. T. "Picturing Terror: Derrida's Autoimmunity." *Critical Inquiry* 33 (2007): 277–290.

Mutsaers, Inge. *Immunological Discourse in Political Philosophy: Immunisation and its Discontents*. London: Routledge, 2016.

Plotnitsky, Arkady. "The Violence of Contamination and the Violence of the Pure." *Cardozo Law Review* 13 (1991): 1207–1213.

Rottenberg, Elizabeth. "The Legacy of Autoimmunity." *Mosaic* 39, no. 3 (2006): 1–14.

Stawarska, Beata. "Derrida and Saussure on Entrainment and Contamination: Shifting the Paradigm from the *Course* to the *Nachlass*." *Continental Philosophy Review* 48 (2015): 297–312.

Teubner, Gunther, ed. *Autopoietic Law: A New Approach to Law and Society*. Berlin: Walter de Gruyter, 1988.

Wortham, Simon Morgan. *The Derrida Dictionary*. London: Continuum, 2010.

Auto (Immunity): Evolutions of Otherness

Nicole Anderson

For Derrida, the word 'deconstruction'

> like all other words, acquires its value only from its inscription in a chain of possible substitutions, in what is too blithely called a 'context' [...] the word has interest only within a certain context, where it replaces and lets itself be determined by such other words as 'écriture', 'trace', 'différance', 'supplement', 'hymen', 'pharmakon', 'marge', 'entame', 'parergon', etc. By definition, the list can never be closed, and I have cited only names, which is inadequate and done only for reasons of economy.[1]

The endless possible substitutions that (in)form or contribute to the deconstructive lexicon, which we know as those neologisms, paleonyms or what Michael Naas calls 'deconstructo-nyms'[2] are also called 'quasi-transcendentals',[3] precisely because they 'are situated at the margin of the distinction between the transcendental and the empirical',[4] or because they displace traditional oppositions by revealing their contingencies and constructions.[5] It is in his later work that Derrida adds to his suite of 'deconstructo-nyms' with the word 'autoimmunity'; a word he draws from the domain of biology and where, he argues, 'the lexical resources of immunity have developed their authority'.[6] As I will elaborate further on, what is interesting is that as a quasi-transcendental the word autoimmunity not only traverses a path between the eschatological and the teleological (between empiricism and transcendentalism), it consequently redefines 'life' as something other than the human as simply bios or materiality (an organicism) but without falling back into a pure humanism or absolute transcendentalism (transcendental signified).

The term, autoimmunity, first briefly appeared in *Specters of Marx* (originally published in French in 1993)[7] and then a year later, again briefly, in *Politics of Friendship* (in French in 1994).[8] However, it is in three subsequent texts that the most sustained discussions of autoimmunity occur. The first is in 'Faith and Knowledge: the Two Sources of "Religion" at the Limits of Reason Alone' (1998), where Derrida uses the deconstructo-nym to unravel the two sources of religion and the contradiction between religion and technology.[9] Second, in a lengthy interview with Giovanna Borradori entitled:

'Autoimmunity: Real and Symbolic Suicides' (2003), Derrida outlines the operations of autoimmunity in and through a discussion not only on terrorism and in particular the September 11 attacks on the World Trade Center and the Pentagon, but on the differences and similarities between the Cold War and Terrorism since 9/11.[10] The third discussion takes place in *Rogues: Two Essays on Reason* (2005).[11] There Derrida uses the notion of autoimmunity to reveal the aporias or internal contradictions of democracy, and demonstrates its operations in and through a number of political examples. Because the word 'autoimmunity' has been taken from the life sciences and medicine, in all of these texts it serves to articulate and reveal the simultaneous protective and threatening practices in which political life and life *in general* operates.[12]

Expositions on the way Derrida has made use of this term in these works have been made by a number of scholars, including Sam Haddad (2009), J. Hillis Miller (2009) and Michael Naas (2008).[13] The aim of this paper is not to repeat these excellent readings but rather to focus specifically on the way Derrida employs the notion of autoimmunity to deconstruct the notion of a 'self-bounded' identity (what Derrida calls *autos* or *ipseity*: autonomy, self-presence, rationality, Reason, auto-mobility and so on), and to argue that Derrida's use of autoimmunity is not simply negative (*pace* Esposito) but a positive force or affirmation of the other both outside and within ourselves. In order to proceed to this latter argument the following section will briefly outline what Derrida means by 'autoimmunity'.

Autoimmunity: a deconstruction

As Derrida explains, the word 'immunity' derives from the Latin '*munus*, root of the common community'.[14] To be '"immune" (*immunis*)' therefore is to be 'freed or exempted from the charges, the service, the taxes, the obligations' of a community. This definition was then appropriated and applied to the canon law of the Christian Church, as well as to secular constitutional or international law. In regards to the latter the appropriation of the word *immunis* – defined originally as 'exemption' – is to this day in effect as parliamentary or diplomatic immunity.[15] In French (c. 1880), 'immune' came to also mean 'free from contagion', and from this it is not a big leap to see how the word 'autoimmunity' entered the domain of biology.[16] In the next sentence of this footnote in 'Faith and Knowledge', Derrida not only elucidates this French etymology, but then links it with the socio-cultural (religion, science, faith and knowledge). In doing so Derrida brings together the Latin and French etymologies and thereby demonstrates the way in which the word autoimmunity serves as a deconstructonym:

> The immunitary reaction protects the 'indemn-ity' of the body proper in producing antibodies against foreign antigens. As for the process of autoimmunization, which interests us particularly here, it consists for a living organism, as is well known and in

> short, of protecting itself against its self-protection by destroying its own immune system. As the phenomenon of these antibodies is extended to a broader zone of pathology and as one resorts increasingly to the positive virtues of immune-depressants destined to limit the mechanisms of rejection and to facilitate the tolerance of certain organ transplants, we feel ourselves authorized to speak of a sort of general logic of autommunization. It seems indispensable for us today thinking the relations between faith and knowledge, religion and science, as well as the duplicity of sources in general.[17]

In articulating a 'general logic of autoimmunization' Derrida makes clear that the word has become part of the deconstructive lexicon and is used as a means to displace, as well as think through, a range of political, ethical, technical and religious oppositional relations. As he argues in 'Autoimmunity: Real and Symbolic Suicides', one of the most entrenched oppositions this quasi-transcendental challenges is that between body and mind (and by association nature and culture, biology and reason, bios and politics, respectively). Thus the word autoimmunity is that which calls into question the unity and purity of any 'body', and any 'concept':

> Enormous effort will be required to introduce here all the necessary distinctions (both conceptual and practical), which will have to take into account the contradictions, that is, the autoimmunitary overdeterminations on which I've been insisting. Despite their apparently biological, genetic, or zoological provenance, these contradictions all concern, as you can see, what is beyond living being pure and simple. If only because they bear death in life.[18]

It is here that Derrida moves beyond the biological definition of autoimmunity; beyond 'natural life' or 'life pure and simple', and extends it to 'life *in general*', that is, beyond *bios* to *bios politikos*.[19] Consequently, Derrida shifts the meaning of autoimmunity away from its dominant understanding in biology or the life sciences where the autoimmune is defined solely in terms of the 'natural' body's immune system attacking not only foreign antibodies but its own immunity, and in effect committing suicide, to demonstrating that not only the body (in the biological sense) but the body politic (our ethics, politics, science, religion, technology, nation-states, democracy and so on) undergo an autoimmune response. In this shift from the simply biological ('natural life') to 'life *in general*' Derrida reveals that life is constituted by the autoimmune. So when Derrida says in the quote above 'death in life', he is also deconstructing the limits between life and death, between bios and politics and technics, and so on. As Michael Naas so eloquently puts it:

> If the term thus came to prominence in a biological discourse or register, it will have attacked in an autoimmune fashion the

> disciplinary boundaries of that discourse in order to now question the very meaning of bios and the limits of life and death.[20]

But what Derrida's re-inscription of the word beyond the purely biological operates to reveal is not only that death is within life, and that life is thus constituted by the autoimmune, but also, that it is not simply a pure suicide (as the biological definition infers) but 'quasi-suicidal'. Derrida thus puts pressure on the distinctions between life and death, zoe and bios, bios and the political, and hence Derrida's re-working of the definition of autoimmunity in 'Autoimmunity: Real and Symbolic Suicides' as the condition where 'a living being, in a *quasi*-suicidal fashion, "itself" works to destroy its own protection, to immunise itself against its own immunity'.[21]

If we recall now the discussion at the beginning of this paper outlining autoimmunity as a quasi-transcendental (precisely because it marks the 'impurity' of the opposition between the biological and the political, nature and culture, and so on), it becomes clearer from the above quote that Derrida uses autoimmunity as a means to deconstruct the notion of suicide in order to reveal the impurity of the opposition life/death.[22] Or as Derrida in *Rogues* puts it: 'Autoimmunity is more or less suicidal, but, more seriously still, it threatens always to rob suicide itself of its meaning and supposed integrity'.[23] Why does it threaten to rob suicide of its meaning and integrity? As we will see in the following section, suicide's meaning is based on the belief that a self or the subject is a unity and self-bounded and thus characterized by pure *autos* or *ipseity*. However, autoimmunity exposes the self to be heteronymous rather than autonomous.

Autos Immunis: the quasi-suicide of Reason

In Greek, *autos* means self or same, while the Latin *ipse* is a direct translation of *autos*. In *Rogues*, Derrida tells us that for reasons of economy he uses ipseity to encapsulate a range of humanist and metaphysical traits, such as, self-presence, essentialism, self-reflection, reason and rationality, and all of the *autos* words that characterise the sovereignty of the I or self-same, such as: autonomy, autotely, autobiography, autofinality, automobility and so on.[24] While ipseity (or throughout his early oeuvre what he calls 'presence' and self-presence) is metaphysically founded, and therefore the *effects of* ipseity are real, nonetheless, Derrida at the same time argues that the self in itself (as that which is 'self-present'/self-same) is a fable because '[t]he relation to self can only be based on difference and not only self-presence'.[25] Before discussing the ways in which autoimmunity exposes ipseity as a fable, and before returning to autoimmunity as *quasi*-suicidal, I want to now turn to one of the characteristics of ipseity, namely Reason-rationality, to demonstrate the way in which the 'self' becomes the 'self-same' and thus immunizes itself from the 'other'.

As Derrida famously demonstrates, Hegel's notion of the relation of 'will' entails the immediate presence to self. It is the self's presence to self in thought, and which is manifested through rationality, reason and therefore self-reflection, that distinguishes the human from the animal and the other more generally (from nature and the biosphere). In other words, rationality and reason (which requires deductive and inductive logic, critical reflection, anaylsis, evaluation, judgement, objective distance and so on) defines the 'human' as that which stands outside and apart from, and thus in control of, itself and what is outside itself: nature and biological systems. A distinction between inside and outside is thereby constitutive of the self's attempt to control and exercise autonomy and sovereignty through rationality.

This form of rationality, one that has traditionally given us the definition of the human per se, is based on a philosophical notion that Reason is the principle of Reason, that is, Reason is *a priori* (in the Kantian or Leibnizian sense). Or as Derrida argues, 'reason, thus, unveils itself [...] It emerges from itself in order to take hold of itself within itself, in the "living present" of its self-presence'.[26] It is only because Reason is the principle of Reason that it can be independent of all empirical, aesthetic (moral feeling) and religious influence, and which is why, for Immanuel Kant, in the individual 'the principle of autonomy is thus the self-possessed legislation of the power of choice through reason'.[27] The principle of autonomy leads to the obedience of the moral law, in and through which humanity attains freedom, sovereignty and Enlightenment, all of which are built on and imbricated in ipseity. While Derrida has been deconstructing 'self-presence' since his earliest works, it is in *Rogues* that he makes the connection between the self-same or self-presence, and sovereignty, democracy and autoimmunity. This connection is made through the metaphor of the wheel (circularity), which is used to demonstrate the way the Self (and Reason) in taking 'hold of itself within itself', requires a turning in on oneself. Derrida argues that 'man' recognises

> oneself as man by returning to oneself in a specular, self-designating, sovereign, and autotelic fashion [...] Indeed, it seems difficult to think such a desire for naming of democratic space without the rotary motion of some quasi-circular return or rotation toward the self, toward the origin itself, toward and upon the self of the origin, whenever it is a question, for example, of sovereign self-determination, of the autonomy of the self, of the *ipse*, namely, of the one-self that gives itself its own law, of autofinality, autotely, self-relation as being in view of the self, beginning by the self with the end of self in view [...] By *ipseity* I thus wish to suggest some 'I can', or at the very least the power that gives itself its own law, its force of law, its self-representation, the sovereign and reappropriating gathering of self in the simultaneity of an assemblage or assembly, being together, or 'living together', as we say.[28]

This turn upon the self by the self is what gives the self its identity (its self-gathering), its sovereignty, its power, and as we will see shortly it is what gives the self a notion of, or teleological trajectory towards, its own end. I would argue then that ipseity, and hence Reason, is a form of 'immunity' that acts to protect itself against the natural (biological) order of which it is a part. It is therefore an immune response to anything that threatens the bounded self (*ipse*). But this turning within itself is not only an immune, but precisely an autoimmune, response: 'Still following the figure of this wheel [*roue*], this route that turns back on itself, this additional turn or twist, this roundness of the turn and of the tower, this return to self, the law of a terrifying and suicidal autoimmunity'.[29] Ironically, as Michael Naas points out, 'the only auto word that does not perpetuate the notion of a unified, whole, and autonomous self is "autoimmunity" that undoes the supposed presence or sovereignty of the self'.[30] That is, by the same means of protecting itself (by forming communities based on reason and rationality in order to produce enlightenment, but thereby distancing humanity from the biological natural world and the effects of human life on the environment through pollution, over population, or by protecting itself from wars, terrorism, the foreigner, etc.), Reason (which characterises the sovereign self), destroys itself: its cure becomes its poison. Or, according to Derrida in the same way that repression works (whether it is psychoanalytic, political, economic), likewise I would argue ipseity 'ends up producing, reproducing, and regenerating the very thing it seeks to disarm',[31] because '[a]utoimmunity is always, in the same time without duration, cruelty itself, the autoinfection of all autoaffection. It is not some particular thing that is affected in autoimmunity but the self, the *ipse*, the *autos* that finds itself infected'.[32] In other words, the self or the 'being of self-identity' is always already autoimmunised, because 'life *in general*', life itself, the *bios*, or the '*bios politikos*', not only admits non-life, but is constituted by the other, the foreign, the alien.[33]

Because, 'life *in general*', *bios*, and political life are always already infected, always already an autoimmune response, and if Reason and hence ipseity are constituted by the autoimmune, then are they simply part, and thus a representation, of a natural code? In other words, is ipseity, and hence Reason, purely a function of biology, or more aptly, evolutionary biology? If so, then 'the only politics possible' as Roberto Esposito argues, when outlining some problems with some aspects of biopolitical discourse, 'will be the one that is already inscribed in our natural code [...] human beings cannot be other than what they have always been. Brought back to its natural, innermost part, politics remains in the grip of biology'.[34] The negative implication of this position of course is that Reason is simply a behaviour, biologically determined, so that not only are any previous and future notions of Enlightenment a fable, along with the notion of the 'self' (*ipse*), but that as a consequence the human race inevitably produces ecological-biological crisis as well as war and terror against each other, and is thus hurtling towards self-destruction, or self-suicide. For Esposito and Cambell, the autoimmune therefore is a purely negative force and response. However, Esposito's claim that 'human beings cannot be other than what they have always been' is based on two humanistic assumptions: first, that there is an essential unchanging core (i.e. 'innermost part') that constitutes the human, and in turn, that this core is biologically determined or constituted as Reason, autonomy, self-presence, in a word, ipseity, and second, that 'our natural code' (genetic code) is the point of origin of mankind, and unfolds along an eschato-teleological evolutionary trajectory towards an end point. Contrary to the understanding of autoimmunity as a negative force, later I will explore the ways in which Derrida sees the positive workings of the autoimmunity of Reason, but before this I want to turn to one of Derrida's early essays 'The Ends of Man' (1986) to explore how the two assumptions just outlined perpetuate humanistic positions.

In this essay Derrida defines the *origin* and *end* of 'man' as such:

> The end of man (as a factual anthropological limit) is announced to thought from the vantage of the end of man (as determined opening or the infinity of a telos). Man is that which is in relation to his end, in the fundamentally equivocal sense of the word. Since always. The transcendental end can appear to itself and be unfolded only on the condition of mortality, of a relation to finitude as the origin of ideality. The name of man [...] has meaning only in this eschato-teleological situation.[35]

For Derrida the 'ends of man' can be defined as the teleological (origin) at one end and eschatological (end) at the other. Therefore, what Derrida is arguing here is that the *thinking* on the ends of man, by man, is enabled in and through the structure of eschatological and teleological reasoning. To think the ends of man is to project and to think about the origins and destination of the human, which in turn perpetuates an '(onto)theological determination [...] which is present in every humanism'.[36] So for Derrida, to be able to think the end in itself – whether or not that end is self-destructive ecological annihilation or self-suicide as Campbell's and Esposito's positions might lead us to conclude – is actually a result of 'man's essence as a rational being, as the rational animal'; it is the type of metaphysical thinking that attempts to raise 'itself above experience, that is, above finitude'.[37] And in rising above finitude 'man' attempts to rise above the purely biological despite the fact that as Claire Colebrook points out, 'biological evolution stresses the absence of any end, form or prima facie determination of life'[38] because, contrary to popular understanding evolution does not unravel towards some given end.[39]

Yet here is the rub, for all this supposed anti-humanism in evolutionary and biological theory (and encapsulated in Esposito's idea that Reason is *perhaps* biological and thus by implication there is no individual autonomy), 'the human' is, nevertheless, 'precisely that being who perceives this absence of end or essence and thus gives itself its own [origins and] ends'.[40] In other words, Campbell and Esposito's supposed anti-humanist questioning and assumptions are nonetheless a perpetuation of the metaphysical-humanist story of the 'ends of man'. It might seem that Derrida is concurring with the idea that there is a 'rational essence'. Derrida does not deny Reason or rationality, but he does challenge the ways in which Reason has been privileged in the history of metaphysics and thus the humanistic perpetuation of a certain kind of Reason (mechanistic) as either biologically or metaphysically 'originating' and unfolding through time and space in an eschato-teleological trajectory. In other words, by traversing in a quasi-transcendental fashion a path between these two 'ends of man', the teleological (origin) and eschatological (end), Derrida is able to deconstruct 'the principle of organization of the structure', which is the construction of a centre and a fixed point of origin, and thus decentre a humanistic thinking. This teleology, in evolutionary terms, is the origin of man as beginning with the genome, all of which Derrida signals as perpetuating a certain form of humanistic thought about the end of man.[41] To put it differently, I am suggesting that Derrida traverses a path between finite (material) and infinite (transcendental) ends, and in evolutionary terms, this means Derrida

> charts a path between [on the one hand] conceiving life as blind quantitative variation that could ultimately be reduced to an algorithm and that would reinforce the Cartesian man of measurement and, [on the other hand] the other extreme that would refer to force, life or power beyond any human or organic principle.[42]

Taking a path between these extremes: between empiricism and transcendentalism, teleology and eschatology, finitude and infinitude, Derrida's quasi-transcendental move not only decentres the humanist thinking on man, but reveals more importantly that 'man' decentres himself, or more aptly, is always already decentred as a result of autoimmunity, precisely because *life*, Derrida argues, can be defined as autoimmunity. For Derrida, then, man is not the origin, or centre, or a determined genetic origin that follows a particular or only one genealogical trajectory (if at all), and this is because the origin of man is always already autoimmune: neither life nor non-life, both life and non-life. Autoimmunity is a means by which to disrupt or question 'the autobiography [and historico-teleological narrative] of the human species' as it is presented in evolutionary-biological forms. As Derrida argues,

> history, historicity, even historicality, those motifs belong precisely [...] to *this* auto-definition, *this* auto-apprehension, *this* auto-situation of man or of the human *Dasein* as regards what is living and animal life; they belong to this auto-biography of man, which I wish to call into question.[43]

An auto-biography that I would argue can be defined as the humanist thinking on the ends of man.

So far Derrida has shown us that man is not the origin, and has employed the deconstructonym, autoimmunity, as a means of revealing the human and thus life as always already autoimmune. Furthermore calling into question the 'ends of man' Derrida is also able to deconstruct a humanist thinking that underpins the biological and the metaphysical. Yet whether or not we believe Reason to be purely biological, or a force/power that takes man beyond finitude and organicism, the question still remains: how do we begin to seek a new mode of thinking or thought not founded on metaphysical knowledge and reason when we always already biologically embody the effects of *ipseity* (that is, autonomy, self-presence, rationality, Reason, automobility)? Derrida's answer to this is in the way we take up or 'respond to the call of the principle of reason'.

Historically or traditionally 'the response to the call of the principle of reason is thus a response to the Aristotelian requirements, those of metaphysics, of primary philosophy, of the search for "roots", "principles", and "causes"'; it is a response, in other words, that utilises a dimension of technical, scientific and philosophical reason or thought and criticism.[44] Notably, for Derrida, responding to this call does not mean either obeying or disobeying this principle. Rather, response entails a broader definition of thought, one that 'would interrogate the essence of reason and the principle of reason, the values of the basic, of the principle, of radicality, of the *arkhe* in general, and it would attempt to draw out all the possible consequences of this questioning'; it is a form of thought that unmasks 'all the ruses of end-orientated reason' in order to produce, in turn, new '"thought" – a dimension that is not reducible to technique, nor to science, nor to philosophy'.[45] Or, as Derrida argues in *Rogues*: 'What must be thought here, then, is this inconceivable and unknowable thing, a freedom that would no longer be the power of a subject, a freedom without autonomy, a heteronomy without servitude'.[46] If, as Derrida argues, responding to the call does not mean either obeying or disobeying the principle of Reason, it is because 'thought requires both the principle of reason and what is beyond the principle of reason',[47] because after all, 'reason is only one species of thought – which does not mean that thought is irrational'.[48] However, once we move away from conventional or metaphysical notions of what is defined as thought, or even reason, while still taking account of the ways in which *ipseity* is embodied, then how to respond, how to think beyond the principle of Reason, becomes more interesting but also more difficult to answer, especially in light of Esposito's claim that response (and hence politics and reason) is biologically encoded. Yet, as Derrida shows us in the next section, his positive re-inscription of autoimmunity not only deconstructs the humanism underpinning both metaphysics and the biological origin discussed earlier, it also offers a way out of this dilemma, and thus at the same time addresses this issue of how to think differently.

The 'other' as life *in general*

On the one hand, Derrida in 'Faith and Knowledge' acknowledges that autoimmunity is a threat because it potentially destroys the immune system that protects the organism from external attack, which is why Derrida's autoimmunity has been interpreted, for example by Tim Campbell, as 'always destructive' and negative.[49] But for Derrida autoimmunity is not simply destructive, because on the other hand, as he argues in *Rogues*,

> autoimmunity is not an absolute ill or evil. It enables an exposure to the other, to *what* and to *who* comes – which means that it must remain incalculable. Without autoimmunity, with absolute immunity, nothing would ever happen or arrive; we would no longer wait, await, or expect, no longer expect one another, or expect any event.[50]

As Michael Naas elucidates, autoimmunity is the 'chance for any living organism'. For example, 'as in the case of immuno-depressants, a chance for an organism to open itself up to and accept something that is not properly its own, the transplanted organ, the graft, in a word, the other, which is but the cutting edge, the living edge, of the self. Without certain forces of autoimmunity, we would reject organs and others essential to "our" survival – whether we are talking about an individual body, a community, or a nation-state', or let me add, in this case, the principle of Reason.[51] Again as Derrida puts it: 'This chance is always given as an autoimmune threat'.[52] Here autoimmunity is a trope for not only the way Derrida deconstructs humanism or Reason from within humanism and Reason, but for the way in which Reason perpetually deconstructs itself. Thus, there is a double move encapsulated in the autoimmune: where as we have seen 'a living being in quasi-*suicidal* fashion, "itself" works to destroy its own protection' by immunizing itself against its own immunity, it is only because of this autoimmunity that the living being has a 'chance', or a means of saving itself by losing itself in opening to the absolute other and thus becoming other.[53] (In this sense autoimmunity works similarly to Derrida's notion of the *pharmakon*, a deconstructo-nym that conveys that which is both poison and cure: the cure is a poison and this poison simultaneously is cure).[54] What we see Derrida doing then is bringing together these two autoimmune paths (the negative: destruction, and positive: opening or chance) in order to demonstrate that there can be no positive without the negative and vice-versa.

When we think of the autoimmune as the 'chance' for any living organism, for 'life *in general*', Derrida's qualifier, 'quasi-suicidal', perhaps now makes more sense. First, because if autoimmunity is constitutive of any self, then there can be no pure or unified self, no self that is not in and of 'itself', other. The autoimmune, that is, reveals the *multiple* conceptual and material autoimmunities that construct the subject, so that in a double move autoimmunity is that which simultaneously deconstructs the 'sovereignty of the self'[55] and the body, thus further undermining, as discussed earlier, the

Cartesian opposition between mind and body; Reason and biology. Second, and consequently, there can be no pure suicide because as Haddad argues there is 'no longer a stable self that can be seen to be putting itself to death, and suicide starts to lose its meaning'.[56] There can only be, I would argue, evolutions of otherness (that do not follow an eschaton-teleological trajectory). In other words, it is precisely this double move encapsulated in the autoimmune that enables an opening to this other form of thinking or thought (away from end-orientated reason). Reason, then, being structured by an autoimmunity, and hence a double move that is quasi-transcendental, is thus always already opened for, with, to the other, that enables a thinking or existence beyond the purely empirical or material. This is not to suggest that the beyond I am talking of here is an absolute transcendentality, or a transcendental signified, and I am not denying materiality or empiricism. Rather, I am suggesting that the beyond is generated, or made apparent, from within materiality ('death within life').

Given this, the way out of the notion that Reason (and hence politics, *bios*, and so on) is simply and only a natural code, and thus purely biological, is to demonstrate as Derrida in fact does, that Reason as an autoimmune response positively contains within itself its own other, and thus its own opening to other modes of thinking and experience. To make the point differently, the exposure to the other, and by 'other' I mean the unexpected, unknown experience of what is to come (whether it be a *who* or *what* to come) – precisely because it is uncalculated and unknown – enables a movement, or an experience, beyond the human as simply materiality. And this experience beyond the human as simply materiality can thus lead to a new means of thinking life apart from the biological and humanist notions of humans. In other words, and ironically, it is precisely this materiality (Reason as biological) that 'may take life beyond its carbon based, intentional and intelligent forms', so that the human biological organism (and hence Reason, rationality, autonomy, etc.) through its own autoimmunity is exposed to differing forms of evolutions or otherness (cultural and technical, for instance) that do not have their *origins* or *end* in necessarily organic materiality.[57]

Consequently, *bios politikos* and political action is not simply, as Esposito argues, inevitably and purely biological as he defines it. Rather, and coming back to the opening paragraph of this paper, I would argue that ipseity (and hence Reason and the political) is quasi-transcendental, that is, simultaneously a result of, embedded in, and beyond purely biological carbon based materiality.

Disclosure statement

No potential conflict of interest was reported by the author.

Notes

[1] Derrida, "Letter to a Japanese Friend," 4-5.
[2] Naas, *Derrida From Now On*, 135.
[3] Quasi-transcendentals can be defined as (non)structures because archewriting, différance, trace etc., can be used interchangeably (as a relation of economy), while also being, at the same time, separate and singular. As Derrida remarks, 'the kind of bringing together proposed here has the structure of an interlacing, a weaving, or a web, which would allow the different threads and different lines of sense or force to separate again, as well as being ready to bind others together' (see Derrida, *Speech and Phenomena: and Other Essays on Husserl's Theory of Signs*, 132). See also Gasché, *The Tain of the Mirror: Derrida and the Philosophy of Reflection*; Bennington and Derrida, "Derridabase." For a detailed discussion of the history of the development of this term and its use by Bennington, Gasché and Rorty see also Kates, *Essential History: Jacques Derrida and the development of deconstruction*.
[4] Gasché, *The Tain of the Mirror*, 317.
[5] Bennington and Derrida, "Derridabase," 279.
[6] Derrida, "Faith and Knowledge: the Two Sources of 'Religion' at the Limits of Reason Alone," 73.
[7] Derrida, *Specters of Marx: The State of the Debt, the Work of Mourning, andthe New International*.
[8] Derrida, *Politics of Friendship*.
[9] The two sources of religion that Derrida refers to include 'the unscathed (the safe, the sacred or the saintly) and the fiduciary (trustworthiness, fidelity, credit, belief or faith, 'good faith' implied in the worst 'bad faith')' (Derrida, "Faith and Knowledge," 63).
[10] Derrida, "Autoimmunity: Real and Symbolic Suicides: A Dialogue with Jacques Derrida."
[11] Derrida, *Rogues: Two Essays on Reason*.
[12] Naas, *Derrida From Now On*, 135.
[13] See Haddad, "Reading Derrida Reading Derrida" and Miller, *For Derrida*; and Naas *Derrida From Now On*.
[14] Derrida, "Faith and Knowledge," 72, n. 27.
[15] Derrida, "Faith and Knowledge," 72, n. 27.
[16] *OED*.
[17] Derrida, "Faith and Knowledge," 72, n. 27.
[18] Derrida, "Autoimmunity," 119.
[19] Derrida, "Autoimmunity," 187, n. 7.
[20] Naas, *Derrida From Now On*, 141.
[21] Derrida, "Autoimmunity," 94.
[22] See Haddad "Reading Derrida Reading Derrida," 517.
[23] Derrida, *Rogues*, 45.
[24] Derrida, *Rogues*, 9-14.
[25] Derrida and Nancy, "'Eating Well,' or the Calculation of the Subject: An Interview with Jacques Derrida." As a quick but relevant aside, what we find in *Rogues* is Derrida making a close association between his neologisms différance and autoimmunity in his earliest and later works respectively. As Naas interprets it, this 'grafting of autoimmunity onto différance' that takes place in *Rogues* enables Derrida to show that democracy not only immunizes itself by marginalizing some aspects of its community, but consequently it is always 'in the name of its own protection and immunization' that 'democracy, defers or adjourns democracy 'itself' to another day' (see Naas, *Derrida From Now On*, 136, see also Derrida, *Rogues*, 35). Hence Derrida's claim that democracy is always 'to come'.
[26] Derrida, *Writing and Difference*, 166.
[27] Kant, "The Metaphysics of Morals," 659.
[28] Derrida, *Rogues*, 10-11.
[29] Derrida, *Rogues*, 18.
[30] Naas, *Derrida From Now On*, 127.
[31] Derrida, "Autoimmunity," 99.
[32] Derrida, *Rogues*, 109.
[33] Derrida, *Rogues*, 45; Naas, *Derrida From Now On*, 129 and 135.
[34] Esposito, *Bios: Biopolitics and Philosophy*, 23-24. See also, Esposito and Campbell, "Interview: Roberto Esposito."
[35] Derrida, "The Ends of Man," 123.
[36] Balibar, "Eschatology versus Teleology: The Suspended Dialogue between Derrida and Althusser," 66.
[37] Derrida, "The Ends of Man," 122.
[38] Colebrook, "Creative Evolution and the Creation of Man," 119.
[39] Wesson, *Beyond Natural Selection*. In neo-Darwin biology theory Wesson says that while 'evolution [...] carries on in a direction that has been adaptive of the past' (192), evolution does not proceed toward a goal, and thus there is no final or overall meaning. For example, Stephen J. Gould and Niles Eldredge's claim that rather than 'gradual' (built on the notion of teleology

and genealogy), there is 'rapid' or 'stasis and punctuation' evolution. Stasis is defined as the dominant and definite lines along which a species evolves, despite the differences that come about through genetic and environmental changes (Wesson, *Beyond Natural Selection*, 148). When a species does adapt through variation to environmental changes and opportunities, this is a result of a sharp punctuation (208). Stasis-punctuation is not opposed to Darwin's theory of evolution, but it does challenge his notion of 'descent with modification' as that which proceeds gradually and continuously. Consequently, 'stasis-punctuation' suggests that the past cannot and should not be understood 'in terms of forces at work in the present' (13). For more on this see Anderson, "Supplementing Claire Colebrook: A Response to 'Creative Evolution and the Creation of Man'".

[40] Colebrook, "Creative Evolution and the Creation of Man," 119.

[41] See both Derrida, "The Aforementioned So-Called Human Genome" and Derrida, *Geneses, Genealogies, Genres and Genius: The Secrets of the Archive*.

[42] Colebrook "Creative Evolution and the Creation of Man," 130.

[43] Derrida, *The Animal That Therefore I Am*, 24.

[44] Derrida, "The Principle of Reason: The University in the Eyes of its Pupils," 8.

[45] Derrida, "The Principle of Reason," 16.

[46] Derrida, *Rogues*, 152.

[47] Derrida "The Principle of Reason," 18-19. See also Derrida, *Writing and Difference*, where he talks about difference being internal to reason itself, what he calls dissension to describe 'a self-dividing action, a cleavage and torment interior to meaning *in general*, interior to logos in general [...] As always the dissension is internal, the exterior (is) the interior, is the fission that produces and divides it' (38-39).

[48] Derrida "The Principle of Reason," 16.

[49] Campbell, "Bios, Immunity, Life: The Thought of Roberto Esposito," 8.

[50] Derrida *Rogues*, 152.

[51] Naas, *Derrida From Now On*, 131.

[52] Derrida *Rogues*, 53.

[53] Derrida, "Autoimmunity," 94.

[54] See Derrida, *Dissemination*.

[55] Naas, *Derrida From Now On*, 127.

[56] Haddad, "Reading Derrida Reading Derrida," 517.

[57] Colebrook, "Creative Evolution and the Creation of Man," 130.

Bibliography

Anderson, Nicole. "Supplementing Claire Colebrook: A Response to 'Creative Evolution and the Creation of Man.'" *Journal of Southern Philosophy*. Spindel Supplemet. 48.S1 (2010): 133–146. Available online: http://onlinelibrary.wiley.com/doi/10.1111/sjp.2010.48.issue-s1/issuetoc

Balibar, Etienne. "Eschatology versus Teleology: The Suspended Dialogue between Derrida and Althusser." In *Derrida and the time of the political*, edited by Pheng Cheah and Suzanne Guerlac. Durham: Duke University Press, 2009.

Bennington, Geoffrey, and Jacques Derrida. "Derridabase" In *Jacques Derrida*. Chicago: University of Chicago Press, 1993.

Campbell, Timothy. "Bios, Immunity, Life: The Thought of Roberto Esposito." *Diacritics* 36, no. 2 (2006): 2.

Colebrook, Claire. "Creative Evolution and the Creation of Man." *Journal of Southern Philosophy*. Spindel supplement. 48.S1 (2010).

Derrida, Jacques, and Jean-Luc Nancy. "'Eating Well', or the Calculation of the Subject: An Interview with Jacques Derrida." In *Who Comes After the Subject?*, edited by E. Cadava, et al. New York, NY: Routledge, 1991.

Derrida, Jacques. "Autoimmunity: Real and Symbolic Suicides: A Dialogue with Jacques Derrida." In *Philosophy in a Time of Terror: Dialogues with Jürgen Habermas and Jacques Derrida*, edited by Giovanni Borradori. Chicago: Chicago University Press, 2003.

Derrida, Jacques. "Faith and Knowledge: the Two Sources of 'Religion' at the Limits of Reason Alone." In *Religion*, edited by Jacques Derrida and Gianni Vattimo. Stanford: Stanford University Press, 1998.

Derrida, Jacques. "Letter to a Japanese Friend." In *Derrida and Différance*, edited by D Wood and R Bernasconi, 4. Evanston: Northwestern University Press, 1988.

Derrida, Jacques. "The Aforementioned So-Called Human Genome." *Negotiations: interventions and interviews 1971-2001*, edited by Elizabeth Rottenberg. Stanford: Stanford University Press, 2002.

Derrida, Jacques. "The Ends of Man." *Margins of Philosophy*. Trans. Alan Bass. Chicago: University of Chicago Press, 1986.

Derrida, Jacques. "The Principle of Reason: The University in the Eyes of its Pupils." *Diacritics* 13, no. 3 (1983): 3–20.

Derrida, Jacques. *Dissemination*. Translated by Barbara Johnson. Chicago: University of Chicago Press, 1981.

Derrida, Jacques. *Geneses, Genealogies, Genres and Genius: The Secrets of the Archive*. Translated by Beverley Bie Brahic. Edinburgh: Edinburgh University Press, 2006.

Derrida, Jacques. *Politics of Friendship*. Translated by George Collins. London and New York: Verso, 1997.

Derrida, Jacques. *Rogues: Two Essays on Reason*. Stanford: Stanford University Press, 2005.

Derrida, Jacques. *Specters of Marx: The State of the Debt, the Work of Mourning, and the New International*. Translated by Peggy Kamuf. New York and London: Routledge, 1994.

Derrida, Jacques. *Speech and Phenomena and Other Essays on Husserl's Theory of Signs*. Translated by David B. Allison. Evanston: Northwestern University Press, 1973.

Derrida, Jacques. *The Animal That Therefore I Am*. Translated by David Wills. New York: Fordham University Press, 2008.

Derrida, Jacques. *Writing and Difference*. Translated by Alan Bass. New York: Routledge, 1978.

Esposito, Roberto, and Timothy Campbell. "Interview: Roberto Esposito." *Diacritics* 36, no. 2 (2006): 49–56.

Esposito, Roberto. *Bios: Biopolitics and Philosophy*. Translated by Timothy Campbell. Minneapolis: University of Minnesota Press, 2008.

Gasché, Rodolphe. *The Tain of the Mirror: Derrida and the Philosophy of Reflection*. Cambridge: Harvard University Press, 1997.

Haddad, Samir. "Reading Derrida Reading Derrida: Deconstruction as Self-Inheritance." *International Journal of Philosophical Studies* 14, no. 4 (2006): 505–520.

Kant, Immanuel. "The Metaphysics of Morals." In *Moral Philosophy from Montaigne to Kant*, edited by J.B. Schneewind. Cambridge: Cambridge University Press, 2003.

Kates, Joshua. *Essential History: Jacques Derrida and the development of deconstruction*. Evanston: Northwestern University Press, 2005.

Miller, J. Hillis *For Derrida*. New York: Fordham University Press, 2009.

Naas, Michael. *Derrida From Now On*. New York: Fordham University Press, 2008.

Wesson, Robert. *Beyond Natural Selection*. Cambridge: MIT, 1991.

(Auto)immunity, Social Theory, and the 'Political'

Cary Wolfe

There's a lot of interest recently in what Roberto Esposito calls the possibility of thinking an 'affirmative' biopolitics that runs counter to the dominant trend in biopolitical thought thus far (thanks in no small part of the work of Giorgio Agamben) – namely, the 'thanatopolitical' cast that seems inevitable when we confront the increasing imbrication of 'life' as a direct object of political power and manipulation. Esposito's key intervention, as is well known, is to insist that the secret to understanding modern biopolitical formations is realizing that their fundamental logic is one of 'immunity' (thus extending an observation that Michel Foucault had already made in his lectures at the Collège de France but had not really developed, at least in Esposito's view). What I want to do here is use the immunological paradigm as a jumping off point to see what new resources for political thought reveal themselves when we return to the isomorphism (if it is one) between the immunological paradigm and the theory of self-referential autopoietic systems handed down to us from second-order systems theory. This will, in turn, open up new lines of connection between the immunological paradigm, systems theory, deconstruction and pragmatism – and will, in particular, reveal some of the ways that social systems theory may be used to extend and refine the work of Foucault himself on biopolitics. When we explore these connections more deeply, they open up avenues to think anew several important questions to which Esposito's work has drawn our attention, including the relationship between community, melancholy, guilt and lack (which, while not thanatological, remains within an ambit that thinks the political in an essentially 'tragic' vein), and the central question that both Esposito and Jacques Derrida quite brilliantly raise: namely, as Esposito puts it, that autoimmunity expresses 'the logic of the immune system in its pure state, so to speak', so that it is not so much pathological as '*non*-pathological or *normally* pathological' – that 'what needs explaining', in other words, 'is not the fact that in some cases the immune system attacks its own parts, but the fact that this normally does not happen'.[1] A crucial problem for politics that we will want to address, then, is the problem of *controlling autoimmunity*. Where this control comes from and what its logic is will lead us on a brief detour through Deleuze's suggestive late remarks on 'control society', again re-articulated here through the apparatus of systems theory, the better to show how what we might call a 'restricted' and indeed 'weak' sense of the political of the sort we find in Niklas Luhmann's work thus has a more complex and fruitful relationship to an understanding of biopolitics focused not on the problem of sovereignty (as in Agamben or Carl Schmitt) but on material *dispositifs* and apparatuses, one that constitutes a much more complex dynamics of political effectivity in an increasingly heterogeneous field of biopolitical actors and agents (not all of them human, of course).

Esposito takes up the immunitary paradigm in many places in his work – not surprisingly, in the most detail in his book *Immunitas* – and he argues that Foucault never really fully develops the immunitary logic of the biopolitical that he identifies in his later work. Foucault recognizes in his lectures from 1976 that 'the very fact that you let more die will allow you to live more',[2] but he is unable to see that the affirmative and thanatological dimensions of biopolitics – either 'a politics *of* life or a politics *over* life', as Esposito puts it – are joined in a single mechanism.[3] For his part, Esposito insists that a turn away from the thanatological workings of biopolitics and toward an affirmative biopolitics can only take place if life as such – not just human (vs. animal) life, not just Aryan (vs. Jewish) life, not just Christian (vs. Islamic) life – becomes the subject of immunitary protection. And this is so, he argues, because 'there is never a moment in which the individual can be enclosed in himself or be blocked in a closed system, and so removed from the movement that binds him to his own biological matrix'.[4] And this leads, in turn, to Esposito's retrofitting of Spinoza's concept of natural right to make 'the norm the principle of unlimited equivalence for every single form of life'.[5] The general idea here is that this new norm will operate as a sort of homeostatic mechanism balancing the creative flourishing of various life forms. As Esposito characterizes it, 'the juridical order as a whole is the product of this plurality of norms and provisional result of their mutual equilibrium'.[6]

Now, while I share Esposito's interest in framing the possibility of an affirmative biopolitics, I also share Eugene Thacker's observation in his book *After Life* that if all forms of life are taken to be equal, then it can only be because they, as 'the living', all equally embody and express a positive, substantive principle of 'Life' not contained in any one of them. 'The problem', he argues, 'is that once one considers something like life-in-itself' – whether in the form of a 'life-principle' or some other 'inaccessible first principle' – then 'one must also effectively dissociate Life from the living'.[7] So I want to come at this question of an affirmative biopolitics and the relations between 'Life', 'the living', and the political by approaching it from a different direction: from the inside out, you might say, rather than the outside in. That is to say, we have to begin at the beginning, with the systems theoretical nature of the immunitary paradigm itself.

As I mentioned earlier, Esposito engages systems theory directly in several places. In *Terms of the Political*, for example, he writes that Luhmann's work 'constitutes the most refined articulation of immunitary logic as a specific form of modernization', which he summarizes along the following lines:

> The problem of systematically controlling dangerous environmental conflicts is resolved not only through a simple

> reduction of environmental complexity but instead through its transformation from exterior complexity to a complexity that is internal to the system itself. To this first strategy of interiorization, however, which is activated by an immunitary process, a second is added which is much more laden with consequences for environmental difference – namely its complete inclusion within the system or its objective elimination. This development in Luhmann's thought, which occurs when he adopts the biological concept of autopoiesis, shifts the lens from the defensive level of the systemic government of the environment to an internal self-regulation of systems that is completely independent and autonomous with regard to environmental pressures.[8]

Without lingering over the rather exaggerated claim 'completely independent and autonomous' that Esposito attributes to Luhmann (wrongly, I think), let me suggest that a better analogy for the systems theory logic of immunity is one that Esposito himself has used elsewhere – namely, the logic of Derrida's *pharmakon*, which 'is opposed to its other not by excluding it, but, on the contrary, by incorporating and vicariously substituting it'.[9]

Let me explain this analogy in a bit more detail. The equivalent of the immunitary *pharmakon* is, in terms of systems theory, the autopoietic system that uses its own self-reference to process overwhelming environmental complexity (which means not 'completely independent' but all *too* dependent), so that, as Luhmann often puts it, when the distinction between system and environment is 're-entered' within the system's own self-referential code, the difference or distinction, as in Derrida's *pharmakon*, is 'the same and not the same.' Moreover, any system must remain 'blind' to this paradoxical fact of its own self-reference if it wants to continue to use that code to process and reduce environmental complexity. The legal system, for example, could hardly admit that both sides of the distinction legal/illegal are in fact a self-produced product of only *one side* of the distinction (namely the legal) – it could hardly admit, that is, that the system is founded on the tautology 'legal is legal' – because that would collapse the distinction on which its operations depend. It's not that people in the legal system don't know this; it's that they must suspend or ignore this knowledge if they want the legal system to function, otherwise there would be no 'ground' (however *ex nihilo* and suspended over a void, as Žižek might say) for distinguishing the legal from the illegal. *We* (or they) as second-order observers can disclose that paradox, but only from the vantage of another system, using another code, which is in turn bound by the same formal logic that governs all autopoietic social systems.

Hence, in these terms, the 'outside', the environment, is always the outside *of* an inside – a fact that is perhaps easier to grasp in biological and evolutionary work on the autopoiesis of perception and consciousness, reaching back to Jakob von Uexkull's work on human and animal *umwelten* and forward to philosophers of mind such as Alva Noë, who reminds us that 'it is not the case that all animals have a common external environment' because 'to each different form of animal life there is a distinct, corresponding, ecological domain or habitat', meaning that 'all animals live in structured worlds'.[10] The famous 'included exclusion' of biopolitical thought – as the very figure of sovereignty *qua* 'state of exception', as both constituting and constituted violence, as immunity *qua* indemnity (as Derrida puts it) and so on – is a product of the 're-entry' of the system/environment distinction within the system's own self-referential frame.

Let me stress two important points that follow from this in closing out this crash course in systems theory: first, this means, as Esposito puts it, that for autopoietic immune systems, the task is not to protect the body *from* conflicts but rather *through* conflicts – indeed (to look forward to the material on control society later in this essay) to use conflict in the system to manage and respond, *in a non-representational way*, to conflicts in the broader environment.[11] Second, this means that the immunitary relation between system and environment always operates on the basis of a radical complexity differential between the environment and any system, which is, in fact, the driver for the system's use of self-referential selection as way to reduce, dampen and slow down the ongoing flood of environmental complexity that threatens at every moment to overwhelm it. Or as Luhmann puts it, 'the system's inferiority in complexity must be counter-balanced by strategies of selection', since it is obviously impossible for any system to establish point for point correspondences in real time between its internal elements and every moment to moment change going on in its environment.[12]

I stress this last point to emphasize the fact that systems theory is anything but a form of solipsism or what Graham Harman and other Object Oriented Ontologists call, in a more Kantian register, 'correlationism' – a charge familiar at least since Jürgen Habermas's famous essay on Luhmann in 1990 in *The Philosophical Discourse of Modernity*. As both Luhmann and Maturana make clear, the veracity of the systems theoretical analysis is not about epistemological adequation to some pregiven state of ontological affairs (whether conceived in realist *or* idealist terms), but is pragmatic; that is to say, it is based on its *functional* specificity. Contrary to the understanding of autopoietic systems as solipsistic, the operational closure of systems and the self-reference based upon it arise as a practical and adaptive necessity precisely because systems are *not* closed: that is, precisely because they find themselves in an environment of overwhelmingly and exponentially greater complexity than is possible for any single system. This is precisely why they have to operate selectively and 'blindly' (as Luhmann puts it). Indeed, the 'second-order' turn, as I have argued elsewhere,[13] is to realize that the more systems build up their own internal complexity through recursive self-reference and closure, the *more* linked they are to changes in their environments to which they become more and more sensitive, which is why a bat or a dolphin – or the legal system – can register a higher degree of environmental complexity than an amoeba that responds only to either gradients of light or dark, higher or lower sugar concentrations, and so on, even though both are autopoietic systems. Or as Luhmann puts it in one of his more Zen-like moments, 'only complexity can reduce complexity'.[14]

What this means – and this has been a key insight since the *first*-order systems theory of Gregory Bateson and others – is that the consequences of a particular event or utterance or act depend less on their semantic or informatic formal characteristics than on the dynamic state of the self-referential system itself (and here one might think of the case of the arrest and trial of Steve Kurtz of Critical Art Ensemble, which surely would have taken a different course pre-9/11 and pre-Homeland Security). Or as Luhmann puts it in *Social Systems*, 'one can think "this rose is a rose is a rose is a rose". But this use of a recursive path is productive only if it makes itself dependent on specific conditions and does not always ensue'.[15] 'Accordingly', he continues, 'a piece of information that is repeated is no longer information. It retains its meaning in the repetition but loses its value as information. One reads in the paper the deutsche mark has risen in value. If one reads this a second time in another paper, this activity no longer has value as information (it no longer changes the state of one's own system), although structurally it presents the same selection'.[16]

What all the foregoing draws our attention to is the intensely *non-generic* and 'transversal' (to use Deleuze's term) character of the 'bio-' of biopolitics in its Foucauldian articulation, how it is essentially a strategic problem for the political, one that is conjugated and reconjugated anew under very specific coordinates and conditions, which may be ontological (in the sense of specific forms of embodiment and articulation with the environment) or sociological and historical, or all three at once (and more, of course). This is why, as Hans-Georg Moeller points out, Habermas was in fact right when he called Luhmann's systems theory 'metabiological', because it 'follows evolutionary biology in denying [...] transcendental agency and free will'. That is to say, by definition, that 'an ecosystem has no center. Evolution does not follow any guidelines or directives given by any of its subsystems'.[17] And in turn, he continues, 'the partial blindness that comes with evolution also implies a certain ethical and pragmatic blindness. Since it is impossible to see everything, it is also impossible to see what is good for all' – a point I'll come back to, hopefully in a non-tragic mode, at the end of my remarks.[18]

Of course, if everything we have just said is true of social systems in the context of modernity understood, in Luhmann's scheme, as a process of functional differentiation into a horizontally distributed, non-hierarchical field of social systems, then it is also true, by definition, of the political system. In this light, we might well view this fact (and Luhmann's theory generally) as a description of what Deleuze in his late remarks called 'control society', not least of all because for Luhmann, as we know, the constitutive elements of social systems are not 'persons' or 'individuals' but *communications* – a central feature of control society that Deleuze borrows from none other than William S. Burroughs. Indeed, for Deleuze, writing on the heels of his book on Foucault, what characterizes societies of control is their shift from 'analog' to 'digital' forms of communication that are smooth and continuous across what were, in disciplinary societies, qualitatively different social sites. As Gregory Flaxman puts it,

> far from concentrating power (in a sovereign) or consolidating it (in social institutions), control corresponds to the vast dissemination of power in spaces that seem increasingly smooth and supple [...] Where modern 'disciplinary' societies aggregated individuals in so many 'analogical' sites ('the factory is a prison, the school is a prison'), control societies develop 'inseparable variations, forming a system of varying geometry whose language is *digital*.[19]

If we understand 'digital' here to mean a logic that is discreet and 'non-representational' but at the same time 'formally isomorphic' across the various social systems – not powered from behind by 'real magnitudes', as Gregory Bateson puts it[20] – then the usefulness of the Luhmannian architecture comes readily into view. In control society, the 'person' or the 'individual' (a semantics that both Luhmann and Esposito, along with Foucault and Derrida, reject) is not constituted, as Gregg Lambert puts it, by 'analogical breaks, or points of intense subjective discontinuity between social institutions,' as is the case right up through Althusser's work on interpellation in ideological state apparatuses, but 'rather undergoes a peculiar process of continuous modulation "like a snake shedding its coils"' (to use Deleuze's enigmatic phrase).[21] Rather than being confined in disciplinary spaces and their protocols of enclosure and regimentation, subjects in societies of control move fluidly from one site to the next; instead of initiations and the guild, we have tele-commuting, distance learning, and online defensive driving courses. This is the sense in which, as it is often said, 'control liberates'. As Eugene Thacker and Alexander Galloway characterize it, 'if the body in disciplinary societies is predominantly anatomical and physiological [...] in control societies bodies are consonant with more distributed modes of individuation that enable their infinite variation (informatics records, databases, consumer profiles, genetic codes, identity-shopping, workplace "biometrics"' and the like. 'Express yourself! Output some data!', they write. 'This is precisely how distributed control functions best'.[22] Luhmann's theory of the 'exclusion' of the concrete individual in social systems gives us an especially incisive account of this logic. As Dietrich Schwanitz summarizes it,

> the individual human being belongs to each of these functionally differentiated subsystems for only short periods of time with only limited aspects of his person depending on his respective role as a voter, pupil, reader, patient, or litigant. It is his fundamental exclusion from society that allows the occasional re-entry of the individual under particular circumstances [...] Modern society develops of semantics of individuality that regards the individual as alien, unfamiliar, unpredictable, and free.[23]

Esposito is indeed right that therefore, for Luhmann, 'with respect to the system one is therefore included by exclusion and excluded by inclusion',[24] and that, in these terms, 'community *is* immunity'.[25]

Here, however, we have to remember the 'metabiological' and 'ecological' aspect of systems theory – and in particular its acentric character and its exponential difference between environmental complexity and systemic autopoiesis. From this vantage, what we might characterize as 'the control of control' comes from the 'outside' understood as the overdetermined complexity differential in favor of the environment versus the system – any system – that would attempt to wholly dictate the actions of those who participate in it. Indeed, as Lambert notes, in societies of control, unlike disciplinary societies, resistance 'does not begin from a site internal to a specific power relation that can become collectivized in the general image of a mythical Humanity that suffers from too much oppression', as in the paradigm of the factory strike. Rather, I am suggesting, 'resistance' in Foucault's sense has to be rearticulated as the 'the control of control' that comes not from an intentional subject engaged in a representational act of defiance – the intentional exercise of freedom ('express yourself!') which is, after all, one of the mechanisms by which control society operates – and not from 'Life' capital L, but rather from the weakness of the political system itself vis a vis the overwhelming complexity of its environment and the autonomy of the other social systems in its environment, which in turn undermines the ability of the political system (or any system) to unilaterally determine what 'life' is, what the 'bio-' of 'biopolitics' is, and so on. So if, with Foucault, 'resistance comes first', and is on the side of 'life', this is simply because environmental complexity – 'noise', as Bateson long ago reminded us – is the only source of new patterns, new information, and, for Foucault, 'new schemas of politicization'.[26]

A more concrete example of how this process unfolds is offered by Levi Bryant's attempt to draw out some of the political implications of Luhmann's work by cross-mapping it with some of terms drawn from Jacques Rancière, Alain Badiou and others. Bryant begins with a distinction taken from the lexicon of these thinkers that Luhmann would reject, but is nevertheless useful in this context, when he writes that

> much of what we often call politics is *governance* rather than politics. Governance consists of the manner in which a larger-scale object [or system, in the terms we are using] strives to maintain its structure or organization in its adventure across time and space by domesticating and regulating the elements of which it is composed [...] Politics, by contrast, challenges the manner in which the larger-scale object counts or fails to count other objects, challenges the status of those objects that animate it as elements, instead announcing themselves as parts, and sets about either severing relations to this larger scale object, demolishing this relation, or reconfiguring it.[27]

He then retrofits Badiou's distinction between 'element' and 'part' to Luhmann's account to draw out the relationship between system and environment and the process of what Foucault calls 'politicization': 'an element or a member of a set', he writes, 'exists only for the system in question, and is defined relationally such that its being consists only in its relations to other elements in the system [...] The *parts* of a system, by contrast, are those other systems out of which a system constitutes its elements, are autonomous entities in their own right, and are always in *excess* of the elements that compose a larger-scale system'.[28] For example, the elements 'professor' and 'student' do not exist outside of the educational system that confers upon them their status and role in the system, but they are nonetheless constituted from other objects and systems, such as the psycho-biological materiality of the beings in question, or even, for that matter, their roles as elements in other systems (say, the economic system, which role might, for example, prevent or otherwise effect their ability to serve as elements in the educational system, and so on).

Or, to take another example offered by Bryant (one that has particular resonance for where I live, near the border between the United States and Mexico), 'illegal immigrants are parts of the U.S. social system but are not counted as elements of this system' – and they might be, even more precisely, included as elements in the economic system as wage earners and consumers but excluded from the political system as voters and rights-holders. 'Mathematically', Bryant reminds us – and this sounds as if it could have come straight from the pages of Luhmann's *Social Systems* – 'there are more *possible* relations among *parts* of a system than are admitted by the organization and *elements* of a system'.[29] Or to put it in Luhmannian terms, the environment is always already exponentially more complex than any system, and it is precisely *because* systems surrender a representational relationship to this fact – the fact that they are not driven from behind by real magnitudes, as Bateson puts it[30] – that they can achieve a measure of what we might call 'soft' durability. For Bryant, then, the political 'takes place when a *part* of an object rises up within *another* object and contests its status as a mere *element* of that object [or system]'.[31] 'Politics', he concludes, thus 'marks the site of the volcanic anarchy that bubbles beneath any social organization thereby announcing the contingency of that order'.[32]

To translate this into Luhmannian language, 'politics' would thus be the difference between the perturbing ability of environmental complexity and the ability of the political system to render that complexity meaningful and productive as an element of its own autopoiesis. This process does not, crucially – and this is the connection to Deleuze's control society thesis – *avoid* or *repress* such conflicts (the conflicts, for example, between the [dis]relation of the role of illegal immigrants as elements of the economic versus political system) but rather, precisely, *stages and generates* conflicts over such issues *within* the political and legal domain the better to 'manage' them, so that those conflicts do not, outside the juridico-political system, go unchecked and run amok. And in so doing, the handling of those conflicts serves an 'immunitary' function for society, as Luhmann puts it, by recoding the difference between 'governing' and 'governed' as the internal difference between 'government' and 'opposition'.[33]

It is precisely here that we find the rather ingenious answer to the question raised by both Esposito and Derrida: how does the political system avoid autoimmune disorder if Derrida is indeed right that democracy is 'suicidal'?[34] The answer, according to Luhmann, is this 're-entry' of the political system's guiding distinction (between governing and governed) *within* the political system itself – what Luhmann calls the strategy of the 'divided top' – as a means to manage conflict by *staging* and *using* conflict (a model to which Chantal Mouffe, among others, is quite attracted for its foregrounding of the constitutive nature of social antagonism, as is William Rasch, who characterizes it as a 'domestication' of the friend/enemy distinction we find much more gravely in the work of Carl Schmitt).[35] In doing so, the political system controls autoimmunity by allowing conflicts within the political system between government and opposition to serve the immunitary function of managing – but in a non-representational way – conflicts in the broader society, where Bryant's 'parts' come from. (After all, who really thinks that debates in the United States Congress or Senate between Republicans and Democrats 'represent' the full complexity of the actually existing composition of society as a whole?) Or to put this in the deconstructive terms of Michael Naas's gloss on Derrida's discussion of democracy and (auto)immunity, 'understood as the rule by a *demos* that cannot, as Aristotle reminds us, rule all *at once*, democracy must devise ways for one part of the people to rule and another part to be ruled *in turn, in alternation, in rotation*, one part followed by another'.[36]

As William Rasch summarizes it in his trenchant study *Sovereignty and Its Discontents*, with this 'bifurcation at the top', which gets temporalized as the 'by turns' of Derrida's 'free wheel' of democracy (as he puts it in *Rogues*),[37] 'the "governed" are both included *and* excluded from the realm of government. That this exclusion, as necessary and inevitable as it may be, is at times felt to be oppressive makes it all the more imperative that it, the exclusion, *not* be camouflaged and *not* be denied'.[38] In contrast to a view of the 'properly' political that thinks that 'one can derive morally correct political institutions from abstract, universal norms', the real challenge takes on a different cast 'if we assume that equilibirial difference can only be achieved as a difference of unities, a heterogeneity based on homogeneity, [and that] then the continuous intellectual challenge becomes one of re-entering difference within unity'.[39] Hence,

> we must envision political and social structures that freely acknowledge the ordering and civilizing power of antagonism,' where 'politics cannot compensate for the lack of unity, but rather, by being its effect, *guarantees* this lack [...] Decisions, in other words, can reflexively affirm their status as decisions, or they can silently deny their contingency and assume the gesture

> of logical subsumption. For Derrida and Lyotard, as for Schmitt, it is the unthought violence of this latter possibility that poses the greatest danger.[40]

Now I hasten to add here, that I don't think we need to buy into Rasch's attempt to assimilate Luhmann's systems theory to Schmitt's position – not least of all because Schmitt's friend/enemy distinction cannot in my view survive Derrida's deconstruction of it, any more than Chantal Mouffe's attempt to assimilate *Derrida* to Schmitt on the basis of constitutive social antagonism is convincing either, for different reasons. And if that is the case, if the friend/enemy distinction does not 'elevate' the political system as not just one system among many, but as *the* most important social system, then we are back to the isomorphism between immunity, ipseity, self-reference and autopoiesis being secured not 'existentially' (to use Rasch's phrase), but logically:[41] in which case, as I said before, sovereignty is not sovereign because it shares the same logical structure – indeed, what Esposito calls the same 'finitude' – as all the other social systems.[42] And so, ironically enough, insofar as we are able to secure a 'proper' (that is to say, self-referential and immune) definition of the political, we will also unavoidably end up with a concept of the political that is 'weak'.

But the political is 'weak' and 'blind' in another more important sense that is not limited to its logical status, one we have already alluded to above in our discussion of 'the control of control': namely, in its inability to overdetermine and steer the autopoiesis of the other social systems – especially, I would add, the economic system. This fact was very much in evidence in the United States in the wake of QE2 and QE3 (the policy of 'quantitative easing') and the various political responses to the 2008 economic crisis, and it is very much in evidence now in the US in the growing realization that 'getting tough on immigration' would in effect economically paralyze cities such as the one where I live – Houston, the fourth largest city in the United States, with a plurality population whose largest fraction is Hispanic. As Hans-Georg Moeller suggests, on this point Luhmann would appear to be in agreement with economists such as John Gray at the London School of Economics, who holds that the free market policies of the IMF, which have tried to impose scientific and rational steering on complex economic ecologies, have not prevented and have perhaps even exacerbated economic catastrophes in countries such as Russia and Argentina. As Gray puts it, 'the idea of modernization to which the IMF adheres is a Positivist inheritance. The social engineers who labour to install free markets in every last corner of the globe see themselves as scientific rationalists, but they are actually disciples of a forgotten cult'.[43]

Moreover, and in more general terms, the political system is weak because, as Michael King and Chris Thornhill point out, in the political system power is in fact divided and communicated between a great number of distinct sites and institutions (such as legislatures, lobbyists, cabinet ministers, protest groups, civil servants, appointees and the like), many of which cannot be directly identified with what we would commonly call 'the state'.[44] But this weakness – its 'loose coupling' to other social systems, you might say – is, in fact, a source of the political system's resilience and durability. As they point out, the vast majority of issues in society 'require neither power nor collectively binding decisions'. Problems such as what investments to choose, deciding on a course of treatment for an illness, choosing which college to attend, and so on 'have no directly political content, and may be regulated respectively in the systems of economics, medicine, art, or law'.[45] Now one might object that the political system does indeed intervene in these systems, in the form of addressing fair access to costly drugs by certain groups of people, let's say, or by taking on corruption or fraud in financial markets. But as Thornhill and King point out, these interventions actually serve to 'elucidate and reinforce the differentiation between one system and another', to make sure, for example, that access to appropriate drugs is based *precisely* on medical need alone and not external factors such as race or gender or class, or that financial loss or profit is produced by factors of economic performance and not by unfair advantages in the market gained by extra-economic means such as insider information. And so, they argue, the application of political power 'thus has its most specific function in the avoidance or obviation of unnecessary structural coupling'.[46] And what this means – to borrow Derrida's phrase – is that democracy may be suicidal but *society* is not, precisely because society is 'ecological'.

This fact about the political may seem frustrating to some, and indeed it is bound to be if you think that the 'properly' political is about eschatology, redemption, authenticity, ontological transformation or self-realization of the human race, and so on. On the other hand, this weak concept of the political, its inability to unilaterally change what happens in the other social systems, may be frustrating when 'our' people are in power – if you don't believe me, talk to those who were enraptured by Obama's election in the US – but it is quite a relief when 'their' people are in power, especially if 'we' think that 'they' are crazy. And that is essentially the situation in the US over the past twenty-five years; half the country thinks the other half is crazy. Not 'we disagree', not 'we support different policies', but 'your version of reality is insane'.

And here, I think we do well to avail ourselves of what thinkers from a range of theoretical and philosophical genealogies have characterized as a 'comic' rather than 'tragic' orientation toward these questions, as in Timothy Campbell's exploration, in conversation with Esposito's work, of what he calls 'the impolitical comedy of conflict'.[47] As Esposito puts it, 'the impolitical would imply neither a weakening nor a discontinuation of attention to the political – but to the contrary, its intensification and radicalization'.[48] While the 'anti-political' only confirms that very thing that it resists, the impolitical is a 'non-opposition' that 'reminds the political of its finitude'[49] – 'not from the point of view of something else which is infinite', but from within the very finitude of the terms themselves.[50] For Campbell, the impolitical thus brings us back to conflict, and 'the difference between the political and the impolitical', he continues, 'is thus located in the distinction between conflict that is neutralized in the political and conflict that is composed and which does not move towards an ultimate synthesis in a political ordering'. The comic orientation then, in his words, 'provides the means for acknowledging in lieu of knowing' – in lieu of the symbolic representation and thus control and capture of conflict. And thus, 'the comic figure does not move in terms of a fated order but offers a space in which previously unthought actions become thinkable'.[51]

This 'impolitical' orientation bears striking parallels with what Kenneth Burke – writing in the 1940s in the face of the rise of fascism *and* the infatuation of many of his New York intellectual friends with the Communist party – called 'comic frames' of acceptance.[52] While tragedy, to quote Northrop Frye, 'seems to lead up to an epiphany of law, of that which is and must be', thus leaving us 'with a sense of the supremacy of impersonal power and of the limitations of human effort',[53] comedy for Burke, as John McGowan characterizes it, 'is pluralistic and tolerant, accepting, albeit ambivalently, the co-existence of others with whom we disagree'. 'Lacking the comic frame,' he writes, 'the *demos* shatters into factions and begins to long for a strong authoritarian leader to bring law and order to the chaotic multiplicity of a pluralistic polity'[54] – which lead us directly, of course, to Hitler's famous Telegram 71, brilliantly analyzed by Esposito as the very apotheosis of autoimmunity run (even more) amok.[55] The comic frame is thus not about sovereignty, and not about the sacrifice and scapegoating that sovereignty by definition entails to secure its own self-identity and ipseity. And crucially, it requires of us 'an acceptance of nature and the body that does not ask to be redeemed by any beyond'[56] – a perspective that Burke will develop into a full-blown 'metabiological' theory of social relations and the body's place in them in *Permanence and Change*.[57] In characteristically iconoclastic terms, Burke rejects the tragic 'perfecting of victimage' that is on display for him, as it is for Esposito's immunitary thanatopolitics,[58] in 'the Hitlerite promoting of social cohesion through the choice of the Jew'.[59] Instead, the comic frame of acceptance favors what he calls 'a shift of emphasis from "good times" to "bad times" as the norm', since 'virtues are by very definition rare and exceptional'.[60] Possessed of the comic frame of acceptance, the critic 'will accept it that the pieties of others are no less real or deep through being different from his', and, in taking account as best he can of his own self-referential biases, foibles, habits and so on, will accept 'the dwarfing of our impatience' by never 'forgetting that men build their cultures by huddling together, nervously loquacious, at the edge of an abyss'.[61]

Here, I think, we find a strong point of connection between Burke's 'comic frame' and systems theory's insistence on the constitutive role of the 'blind spot' of autopoiesis and observation, one that allows us to skirt the problems associated with Burke's humanism: namely that adopting 'comic frames of acceptance' can readily sound like simply a matter of taking thought and having a good attitude. For Burke, as McGowan puts it,

> by generalizing guilt, by making us all responsible for the abiding fact of conflict and disagreement, by accepting that all of us retain differences that are not fully compatible with the prevailing order, the socialization of losses eschews the fantasy that one great purgative killing could save us from the slings and arrows of our daily interactions, from the inefficiencies of democracy. Where tragedy trains our focus on 'the individual hero' who attains a kind of 'divinity' through serving as the sacrificial victim, comedy 'replaces' the hero with 'a collective body.'[62]

Here, in all its mundanity, is systems theory's point that 'collective guilt' issues from the fact that all observations are contingent, selective, blind and bound by the fact of their own self-reference – but with the crucial proviso that for systems theory (*and* for deconstruction, *and* for Esposito) the 'person' and the 'individual' are not constitutive elements of the social system as they are for Burke's humanism.

Does this blindness have fatal implications for the comic perspective on the political? I think not. Indeed, in a way, it is a condition of its possibility. It may be true, as McGowan puts it, that 'comedy of the secular, mundane variety' requires 'an acceptance of finitude and a belief in the possible effectiveness of action', but this need not mean that action and affirmation are simply a matter of 'taking thought' – and that is precisely why we need a radically impersonal theory of the social, one accompanied by a requisite theory of social complexity and its complex ecology in which the intentionality of political effectivity is always already embedded. Rather, it means it is a matter of doing the impossible, acting on the basis of contingencies, not grounds. But when viewed in 'metabiological' terms (a label that Burke used for his own approach long before Habermas used it on Luhmann), when we reconceptualize the 'collective body' of the social in these 'ecological' terms, then this blindness is not what prevents political action and affirmation, it is what makes them possible.

Notes

1 Esposito, *Immunitas*, 164.
2 Foucault, "*Society Must Be Defended*," 255.
3 Esposito, *Bios*, 32. Emphasis added.
4 Ibid., 188.
5 Ibid., 186.
6 Ibid., 187.
7 Thacker, *After Life*, 234. For my further reservations, see Wolfe, *Before the Law*, 59-60.
8 Esposito, *Terms of the Political*, 41.
9 Esposito, *Immunitas*, 127.
10 Noë, *Out of Our Heads*, 43.
11 Esposito, *Immunitas*, 47.
12 Luhmann, *Social Systems*, 25-26.
13 Namely, in Wolfe, *What Is Posthumanism?*
14 Luhmann, *Social Systems*, 26.
15 Ibid., 61.
16 Ibid., 67.
17 Moeller, *The Radical Luhmann*, 70-71.
18 Ibid., 72.
19 Flaxman, "The Unfinished Business of Control," n.p.
20 Bateson, *Steps to an Ecology of Mind*, 373.
21 Lambert, "How 'Power Makes Us See and Speak'," n.p.
22 Galloway and Thacker, *The Exploit*, 53.
23 Quoted in Wolfe, *What Is Posthumanism?*, 115.

[24] Esposito, *Immunitas*, 47.
[25] Ibid., 50.
[26] Foucault, "Power Affects the Body," 211.
[27] Bryant, "Of Parts and Politics: Onticology and Queer Politics," n.p.
[28] Ibid.
[29] Ibid.
[30] Bateson, *Steps*, 373.
[31] Bryant, "Of Parts and Politics," n. p.
[32] Ibid.
[33] King and Thornhill, *Niklas Luhmann's Theory of Politics and Law*, 72.
[34] Derrida, *Rogues*, 33.
[35] Rasch, *Sovereignty and Its Discontents*, 6, 8.
[36] Naas, *Derrida from Now On*, 136.
[37] Derrida, *Rogues*, 13.
[38] Rasch, *Sovereignty and Its Discontents*, 9.
[39] Ibid., 147.
[40] Ibid., 41.
[41] Ibid., 92.
[42] Esposito, *Immunitas*, 174.
[43] Quoted in Moeller, *The Radical Luhmann*, 27-8.
[44] King and Thornhill, *Niklas Luhmann's Theory of Politics and Law*, 77.
[45] Ibid., 70.
[46] Ibid., 71.
[47] Campbell, "Genres of the Political," n.p.
[48] Esposito, "Preface to *Categories of the Impolitical*," 102.
[49] Ibid., 104.
[50] Ibid., 103.
[51] Campbell, "Genres of the Political," n.p.
[52] Burke, *Attitudes Toward History*, 170.
[53] Quoted in McGowan, *Pragmatist Politics*, 149.
[54] McGowan, "Kenneth Burke," 245.
[55] See Esposito, *Bios*, 116.
[56] McGowan, *Pragmatist Politics*, 153.
[57] See in particular the 1984 afterword to Burke, *Permanence and Change*, 295-336.
[58] See Esposito, *Bios*, 115-117.
[59] Burke, *Permanence and Change*, 284.
[60] Burke, *Attitudes Toward History*, 120, 114.
[61] Burke, *Permanence and Change*, 272.
[62] McGowan, *Pragmatist Politics*, 182.

Bibliography

Bateson, Gregory. *Steps to an Ecology of Mind*. New York: Ballantine Books, 1972.

Burke, Kenneth. *Attitudes Toward History*. Berkeley: University of California Press, 1984.

Burke, Kenneth. *Permanence and Change*. Berkeley: University of California Press, 1984.

Bryant, Levi. "Of Parts and Politics: Onticology and Queer Politics." Unpublished mss.

Campbell, Timothy. "Genres of the Political: The Impolitical Comedy of Conflict." Unpublished mss. Accessed 29 November 2015. http://www.biopoliticalfutures.net/viewer/index.html

Derrida, Jacques. *Rogues: Two Essays on Reason*. Translated by Pascale-Anne Brault and Michael Naas. Stanford: Stanford University Press, 2005.

Esposito, Roberto. *Bios: Biopolitics and Philosophy*. Translated with an introduction by Timothy Campbell. Minneapolis: University of Minnesota Press, 2008.

Esposito, Roberto. *Immunitas: The Protection and Negation of Life*. Translated by Zakiya Hanafi. London: Polity, 2011.

Esposito, Roberto. "Preface to *Categories of the Impolitical*." Translated by Connal Parsley. *Diacritics* 39: 2, (Summer, 2009): 99-115.

Esposito, Roberto. *Terms of the Political: Community, Immunity. Biopolitics*. Translated by Rhiannon Noel Welch. New York: Fordham University Press, 2013.

Flaxman, Gregory. "The Unfinished Business of Control." Unpublished mss. Accessed 29 November 2015. http://www.biopoliticalfutures.net/viewer/index.html

Foucault, Michel. "Power Affects the Body." *Foucault Live: Collected Interviews 1961-1984*. Edited by Sylvere Lotringer, New York: Semiotexte, 1989.

Foucault, Michel. *'Society Must Be Defended': Lectures at the Collège de France, 1975-1976*. Translated by David Macey and edited by Mauro Bertani and Alessandro Fontana. New York: Picador, 2003.

Galloway, Alexander and Thacker, Eugene. *The Exploit: A Theory of Networks*. Minneapolis: University of Minnesota Press, 2007.
King, Michael, and Thornhill, Chris. *Niklas Luhmann's Theory of Politics and Law*. London: Palgrave, 2005.
Lambert, Gregg. "How 'Power Makes Us See and Speak'." Unpublished mss. Accessed 29 November 2015. http://www.biopoliticalfutures.net/viewer/index.html
Habermas, Jürgen. *The Philosophical Discourse of Modernity: Twelve Essays*. Translated by Frederick G. Lawrence. Boston: MIT Press, 1990.
Luhmann, Niklas. *Social Systems*. Translated by John Bednarz, Jr. with Dirk Baecker. Stanford: Stanford University Press, 1995.
McGowan, John. "Kenneth Burke." *Minnesota Review* 58-60, (Spring and Fall 2002/2003): 241-249.
McGowan, John. *Pragmatist Politics: Making the Case for Liberal Democracy*. Minneapolis: University of Minnesota Press, 2012.
Moeller, Hans-George. *The Radical Luhmann*. New York: Columbia University Press, 2012.
Naas, Michael. *Derrida from Now On*. New York: Fordham University Press, 2008.
Noë, Alva. *Out of Our Heads: Why You Are Not Your Brain and Other Lessons from the Biology of Consciousness*. New York: Hill and Wang, 2009.
Rasch, William. *Sovereignty and Its Discontents*. London: Birkbeck Law Press, 2004.
Thacker, Eugene. *After Life*. Chicago: University of Chicago Press, 2010.
Wolfe, Cary. *Before the Law: Humans and Other Animals in a Biopolitical Frame*. Chicago: University of Chicago Press, 2013.
Wolfe, Cary. *What Is Posthumanism?*. Minneapolis: University of Minnesota Press, 2010.

Index